BSA M20 & M21

Owen Wright

CONTENTS

ISBN 0 85429 485 6

A FOULIS Motorcycling Book

First published 1985

© **Haynes Publishing Group**

Published by:
Haynes Publishing Group,
Sparkford, Nr. Yeovil,
Somerset BS22 7JJ

Haynes Publications Inc.
861 Lawrence Drive, Newbury Park, California 91320 USA

British Library Cataloguing in Publication Data

Wright, Owen
 BSA M20 & M21 Super Profile.—(Super Profile)
 1. BSA motorcycle—History
 I. Title   II. Series
 629.2'275   TL448.B2
 ISBN 0–85429–485–6

Library of Congress Catalog Card Number

85-81460

Editor: Jeff Clew
Page layout: Peter Kay
Jacket colour illustration and photographs: Andrew Morland
Road test: Motor Cycling, courtesy of EMAP National Press Ltd.
Printed in England by:
J.H. Haynes & Co. Ltd

Titles in the *Super Profile* series
Ariel Square Four (F388)
BMW R69 & R69S (F387)
Brough Superior SS100 (F365)
BSA A7 & A10 (F446)
BSA Bantam (F333)
BSA Gold Star (F483)
Honda CB750 sohc (F351)
Matchless G3L & G80 (F455)
MV Agusta America (F334)
Norton Commando (F335)
Norton International (F365)
Norton Manx (F452)
Sunbeam S7 & S8 (F363)
Triumph Thunderbird (F353)
Triumph Trident (F352)
Triumph Bonneville (F453)
Velocette KSS (F444)
Vincent Twins (F460)

AC/Ford/Shelby Cobra (F381)
Austin A30/A35 (F469)
Austin-Healey 'Frogeye' Sprite (F343)
Chevrolet Corvette (F432)
Ferrari 250 GTO (F308)
Fiat X1/9 (F341)
Ford 100E Anglia, Prefect & Popular (F470)
Ford Cortina 1600E (F310)
Ford GT40 (F332)
Jaguar E-Type (F370)
Jaguar D-Type & XKSS (F371)
Jaguar Mk 2 Saloons (F307)
Jaguar SS90 & SS100 (F372)
Lancia Stratos (F340)
Lotus Elan (F330)

Lotus Seven (F385)
MG Midget & Austin-Healey Sprite (except 'Frogeye') (F344)
Mini Cooper (F445)
Morris Minor Series MM (F412)
Morris Minor & 1000 (ohv) (F331)
Porsche 911 Carrera (F311)
Rolls-Royce Corniche (F411)
Triumph Stag (F342)

Bell U-H1 (F437)
B29 Superfortress (F339)
Boeing 707 (F356)
Grumman F8F Bearcat (F447)
Harrier (F357)
Hawker Hunter (F448)
MIG 21 (F439)
Mosquito (F422)
Phantom II (F376)
P51 Mustang (F423)
Sea King (F377)
SEPECAT Jaguar (F438)
Super Etendard (F378)
Tiger Moth (F421)
Vulcan (F436)

Deltics (F430)
Great Western Kings (F426)
Gresley Pacifics (F429)
Intercity 125 (F428)
King Class (F426)
V2 'Green Arrow' Class (F427)

Further titles in this series will be published at regular intervals. For information on new titles please contact your bookseller or write to the publisher.

FOREWORD

It must certainly delight many enthusiasts to see the BSA M20 and M21 side valve singles added to the Foulis Super Profile series.

The M20 and M21 were the last of a long line of simple and sturdy motorcycles that had always been provided by BSA ever since their first motor bicycle appeared in 1910. The kind of ever dependable slogging power offered by the M-type BSA rendered it a must for sidecar users and a favourite amongst even the most discerning motorcyclist who wished for cheap and reliable transport for getting to work and for touring at the weekends.

The Birmingham Small Arms Company was first formed in 1861 when an association of gunsmiths banded together to, 'make guns by means of machinery' and win government and overseas armament contracts. The Company adopted a 'piled arms' trademark and it became a symbol universally renowned for good quality and reliability. When the nations of the world were not at war, the company turned its Small Heath factory towards more peaceful products and began making parts for the bicycle industry and eventually, motorcycles. Yet it was because of the second World War that the M20 gained immortal fame as the khaki-drab British Army standard issue motorcycle. In post-war years the larger capacity M21 gained equal fame in the bright daffodil yellow colours of the Automobile Association. Both models also served with police forces, fire brigades, the GPO, street vendors and countless tradesmen. When the last batch of M21s left the Small Heath works, the golden years of BSA were over and the company slid into a fatal decline. Today, however, the M20 and M21 singles remain a legacy of a byegone age and just how can we forget them! The British army left hundreds, perhaps thousands, of WD-type M20s strewn across the old empire, many of which still provide everyday transport in those distant lands. At home the M-type BSA was the only freely-available motorcycle during the austere post-war days and for many years yet, a BSA side valve single will continue to be unearthed from some old outbuilding or be exposed to daylight once more as a result of another garage clearout.

I'm certain that the following pages will provide a guiding light on one of the most prodigious British four-stroke singles, help those who have inadvertently stumbled upon the remnants of an old slogger, and assist those M20/M21 riders of old to relive the character of a large side valve single, for there must be many!

The 'Owners View' section of any Super Profile book gives the Author a chance to tear himself away from the typewriter and track down enthusiasts who are willing to have their views printed for all to read. Both riders interviewed for the M20/M21 story went much further than merely giving short and sweet answers to the questionnaire. Gordon Jeal not only recalled many of his first-hand experiences with M-type BSAs but also supplied a mass of information including many details that have previously been overlooked. I was stunned with disbelief when Gordon told me about the saga of the ton-up M20. Pete Disson, the WD M20 rider, also kindly loaned me a selection of good quality photographs and an ex-army manual that listed all the dimensions for every intricate detail.

Thanks also go to Barry (Polly) Palmer, bespoke proprietor of Bri-Tie Motorcycles of Swindon, who sent on some items from his collection of ex-factory prints. I am also grateful to Bert Smith of Easton, Nr. Wells, Somerset and to Steve Dickens of Plymouth who so kindly made their machines available for photography.

Over the years I have written numerous articles about the legendary Automobile Association Road Service Outfit so it was a pleasure to correspond once more with Bob Davis of Livingstone, Mid-Lothian to exchange information and stories about these fascinating and incredibly durable outfits. Bob actually owns a couple of ex-AA RSOs still in their original livery and has been given special dispensation by Fanum House to display the AA decals at old vehicle meetings. The AA themselves have never let me down when I've made my requests for photos and my sincere thanks go to Robert Blower and Tim Jackson for delving once again into the Fanum House archives.

To all the M20 and M21 riders that I have met along the way, may your oil pumps never falter! I hope this book will express my gratitude. I've enjoyed my sojourn with the side valve BSA, it's wonderful how such a humble old motorcycle can bring together all sorts of people.

Owen Wright

HISTORY

BSA's very popular M20 and M21 side valve singles were first introduced for the 1937 season as part of a complete new range of 'M' type heavyweight models designed for the company by Valentine Page, a then newly-appointed Chief Design Engineer at the Small Heath works.

The M group were made up of five models given the numerical sequence M19 to M23. Beginning with a 350cc ohv M19 'sports', there then followed the two side valve 'tourers', a 500cc M20, intended for solo and medium sidecar work and the larger 600cc M21 that was more suitable for hauling larger family or tradesmens' sidecars. To complete the array there was a 500cc ohv M22 'Tourer' with a super-sporty M23 'Empire Star' version.

Generally, the M group models all shared the same frame, forks and cycle parts and the engines all had the same basic crankcase assembly. It was all quite a change from the previous year; anyone wishing to buy a BSA in 1936 would have been faced with a bewildering selection of models to choose from, all with various types of styling, lubrication systems and controls. In particular, the mid-range of 350cc to 550cc machines were a complexity of designs that went back to the old 'sloper' singles of the mid 1920s. Even the more recently introduced 'high cam' single cylinder class didn't live up to expectations but instead made the spares stocking situation worse. Some drastic measures were thereby called for to streamline the range and bring about a higher proportion of interchangeable parts.

As early as 1935, the BSA board of directors had anticipated Adolf Hitler's rather bombastic attitude towards the structure of Europe and there began a programme of stockpiling armaments and munitions even in the face of an indifferent government and no forthcoming armament contracts. This may well have been another reason for the company to re-appraise its motorcycle manufacturing policy in 1936, the first step of which was the appointment of Val Page.

Page was one of the most talented and highly respected design engineers in the British motorcycle industry. His early career had been spent at J.A. Prestwich, the world-famous manufacturers of proprietary JAP engines, after which he had moved to the Midlands to work in the drawing offices of Triumph and Ariel. The Page designs of the mid-1930s were noted for their aesthetic style and based on sound engineering principles. The M-type BSAs were certainly no exception to his creativeness.

The design layouts drawn up by Page during 1936 clearly showed the influence of his previous work at Triumph and Ariel. A dry sump lubrication system was favoured for the engine, a steel fabricated oil tank positioned near the rider's saddle had the feed and return oil pipes kept neatly out of the way. The unit was characterised by a long and slowly curving timing cover jutting upwards behind the cylinder barrel and a rectangular tappet inspection cover sitting at the base of the cylinder. Overall, the engine took on a short and stocky shape with clean and uncluttered lines.

Val Page's design layouts were taken up by Herbert Perkins, a long-serving member of the Small Heath drawing office and its Chief Draughtsman throughout the 1930s and the immediate post-war era. He assisted with much of the detail design and ensured that the BSA code of practice was adhered to. The contribution made by Perkins to BSA's successful motorcycles at this time has always been underestimated.

For the M20, a cylinder bore of 82mm was selected, with a stroke of 94mm, giving a swept volume of 496cc. At first, the M21 had a configuration of 85mm x 105mm, to produce a capacity of 595cc, but after just one year in production it was amended to 82mm bore and 112mm stroke, resulting in a slightly smaller engine size of 591cc. Even before the M21 was altered, the actual detail differences between the two engines were few. The M21 had heavier flywheels to cope with the longer crankshaft throw and give the required characteristics for a low-rev, high torque sidecar pulling motor.

BSA had always used letters to designate their various models and throughout the 1930s the letters represented bore and stroke configurations. The initial M21 dimensions of 85mm x 105mm had also been used for the old oil-in-sump model M10 of 1936, hence the reason for the 'M' nomenclature.

The BSA M-type side valve engine earned a reputation for having a very strong and rigid bottom end assembly. The aluminium alloy vertically-split crankcases were well proportioned with ample wall thickness. On the early engines, the crankshaft was supported upon two roller bearings, with an additional outer ball bearing on the drive side. The crankshaft was the customary built-up type with the mainshafts pressed and riveted into the flywheels. A crankpin holding the two flywheels together by taper and nut was fitted, with a double row roller big end. The connecting rod had a forged steel 'I' section with a hardened steel ring pressed into the big-end eye to permit the rod to be reconditioned. Inside the cylinder, an aluminium alloy piston carried two compression rings and one lower slotted oil scraper ring. A fully-floating gudgeon pin was retained in the piston with circlips. A detachable cast-iron cylinder head, with a copper-asbestos gasket, was fastened down onto the barrel using eight bolts, an extra plug bolt being positioned over the cylinder to enable the piston to be set in position for timing purposes. The cooling fins all ran parallel 'fore and aft' across the casting.

Following general time-honoured practice, the valve and timing gear lay on the right-hand side of the engine and consisted of a train of no less than five gears (discounting the internal drive mechanism within the Magdyno). Separate inlet and exhaust cams were driven by the crankcase pinion, each cam spindle supported in bronze bushes between the crankcase and the outer timing cover. The inlet cam gear drove a large idler gear sitting on a fixed spindle and this operated a Lucas M01 Magdyno unit that was bolted onto a platform behind the cylinder barrel. Each cam operated a flat faced tappet that was offset to induce rotation of the tappet and promote even wear. Steel tappet guides were screwed into the crankcase with special tight-fitting threads to prevent loosening. Both tappets carried an adjustable hexagonal head that acted directly onto the valve stems; the exhaust tappet head was shouldered to accept a cable-operated decompressor lever. The inlet valve had a slightly larger head diameter than the exhaust. On the early engines, two valve

guides for each valve were provided, with a gap in between them to encourage heat dissipation.

Dry sump lubrication was the real benefit to be gained from the new BSA engine. At the bottom of the timing side crankcase a rotund 'bulge' was formed in the casting to accept a double-stage gear oil pump driven by a worm on the crankshaft. The upper pair of gears drew oil from the tank and fed it directly into the big end bearing through a relief valve. Once the oil had been thrown by the flywheels on to the cylinder wall, it drained down into a small sump to be collected by the lower stage of the pump and delivered back to the tank. Oil drillings in the crankcase and outer timing cover provided a bleed off from the main pressure supply to lubricate the timing gear. It was a really excellent and reliable oiling system, although some models had an oil pressure indicator button in the instrument panel.

A new engine unit for BSA's latest breed of large calibre singles was all that was required at the time. The buying public were always wary of new models that had too many radical changes, so apart from the external oil tank, most of the cycle parts were based on existing Small Heath practice. The frame was a typical arrangement with a rigidly supported rear wheel and girder fork front suspension. Structurally,

it consisted of tubular sections bolted together through forged lugs that were both pinned and brazed to the tubes. Two of the tubes ran beneath the engine on either side and were then joined to a single tubular member that ran down from the steering headstock to form the main engine and gearbox support cradle. Due to the oil pump 'bulge', the lower right-hand rail had a kink formed into it and for this reason it became a rare sight to see an M20 or M21 engine fitted into another type of frame. As if to pre-empt the intended use of the new side valvers, sidecar fitting lugs were made an integral part of the frame.

The constant mesh, four-speed gearbox was also based on one of BSA's previous models. It had, in fact, originated from the ohv Blue Star of 1932. It was renowned for its smooth gear change operation achieved by ratchet plate mechanism, and the strong casing proved unburstable, to help BSA gain many notable victories in trials events.

On the drive side, a pressed steel oil bath chaincase linked the engine and gearbox units. Shock loads were absorbed by a crankshaft-mounted four-lobe cush drive unit. The clutch fitted for the first year was a single spring, eight friction disc device that had already been in use on the 1935-36 'Empire Star' models. This particular clutch was designed to run dry, so a pressed steel 'cake tin' cover was screwed to the clutch sprocket.

The famous BSA green was applied to the fuel tank, even though it had evolved into a darker Brunswick Green highlighted by a gold stripe running along the brow of the tank. All the rest of the frame and forks were painted black, with plated fittings. A hand lever gearchange, parallelogram silencer with a fishtail end piece, and an instrument panel set into the fuel tank, were features both standard and fashionable at that time.

The 1937 range was put on view for the first time at the Olympia Show in October 1936. Visibly, the only difference between the M20 and M21 was that 3.50 x 19 inch Dunlop Universal tyres had been fitted to the M21 instead of the slimmer 3.25 x 19 inch covers for the M20. The rear wheel was quickly detachable with a 7 inch diameter x 1^3/$_8$ inch wide brake like the front wheel, and both hubs ran on adjustable tapered roller bearings. There was also a spring-up rear stand and for sidecar users, the front brake had a ratchet lever. Priced at £58 for the M20 and £61 for the M21, BSA were offering a fully-equipped machine that represented extremely good value for money. A speedometer was then considered an extra but eventually became compulsory in late 1937.

The M20 and M21 were intended for quite a wide spread of road users. Street vendors, tradesmen and numerous uniformed organisations created the bulk demand for motorcycles that offered endless slogging power and could be maintained with just a few basic tools. It was the sidecar men who also spent their hard-earned cash on cheap but rugged machinery such as the M20 and M21. They will always be remembered as a hardy breed of characters, family men with well-weathered faces and usually seen wearing the obligatory storm coat, wellingtons and a flat cap. Sitting astride a hefty, thumping side valve single the rider must have felt slightly envious of the overhead valve and multi-cylinder boys roaring past, but at least he could enjoy a certain amount of peace without the worry of having the valve gear clattering precariously above the cylinder. With the wife and children huddled away in the sidecar he could, maybe, whistle a tune to the steady bark of the exhaust. Many will agree that the side valve engine had something of the steam age aura about it.

BSA were not without rivals for such a lucrative market. Other factories competed strongly and notable competitors included the Ariel VB, a 600cc machine that had also been designed by Val Page during the early 1930s. The specification of the VB Ariel followed closely that of the M21 but was a little more expensive to buy. It sold on the basis of having the highly revered Ariel badge on its tank; allegiance to one particular manufacturer amongst the motorcycling fraternity was rife. Norton motors had been producing a 500cc model 16H and a 600cc 'Big Four' for many years. Even though the 16H eventually gained a very sporty alloy cylinder barrel, the Norton models couldn't meet their BSA counterparts on price and along with the Ariel VB they were never built in the same large quantities.

Performance-wise, a claimed 13bhp for the M20 and 15bhp for the M21 was hardly likely to lead to any success on the race track but a flat power curve ensured that 55mph could be held all day no matter what gradient or load. Top speed was about 60mph for the M20; the M21 on sidecar gearing could reach just over 50mph. Naturally, it was the more glamorous ohv models that stole the column inches in the Olympia Show reports but then, BSA had their own ways of attracting publicity.

In early February 1938 an attempt was made on the Maudes Trophy, organised by the Auto-Cycle Union and awarded to the factory that put on the most impressive demonstration of durability. Having been issued with a list of 1,000 BSA dealers, the ACU selected at random an M23 Empire Star and an M21 shackled to a BSA sidecar. Under intense observation, the programme of events started with a trip to Wales for 20 non-stop climbs of the dreaded Bwlch-y-Groes mountain pass, then back to London for a stint of speed work which saw the M21 outfit complete 100 laps of Brooklands at an average of 46mph and a flying kilometre sprint timed at 56.26 mph. A return trip to Bwlch for another 20 climbs followed, before criss-crossing London during rush hour with the gear lever locked in top gear. The final coup-de-grace was an engine and gearbox stripdown to undergo a detailed inspection. The ACU officials reported no appreciable wear of any component. The final result saw 1450 punishing miles completed without any mechanical mishaps to earn an outright Maudes Trophy win. Suitably impressed, the Automobile Association placed a large order with BSA and plumped for the 500cc M20 to power their new Road Service Outfits, so beginning a long and glorious acquaintance with the side valve BSA.

1939 had seen quite a number of detail changes to the M20 and M21 engines. There was a new 10 bolt cylinder head and a revised timing gear arrangement. A new six spring clutch had been fitted in the previous year. The multiple springs allowed the fabric insert friction plates to be set up without any tilt and reduce low speed drag. 1939 also saw the introduction of a gentlemanly de-luxe version of the M20 and another stab at the coveted Maudes Trophy. Once more, the stunt involved an M21 combo undergoing another severe test of mountain climbing and London rush hour commuting, locked in top gear. Although the Trophy didn't return to the Small Heath boardroom, the ensuing publicity boosted both sales and reputation. By the spring of 1939, BSA were already receiving plenty of orders not only for motorcycles but for all kinds of military hardware.

Ever since the Great War, BSA had always had close dealings with the War Office and in 1932 the company had designed and built an ohv V-Twin specifically for the Army and RAF. Changes in top personnel at the War Office in 1937 altered general policy in favour of a 500cc single cylinder side valve engine. BSA and Norton were invited to tender for new contracts, Norton submitting their model 16H and BSA putting forward the M20. Both types were accepted after undergoing 10,000 strenuous miles of reliability testing.

In the light of the 1938 Munich crisis BSA accepted a government proposal that it should build up stocks of motorcycles that would eventually be purchased if the necessity arose. Some 3,000 machines were made ready, of which the larger proportion consisted of M20 and M21 types. Other nations were also eager to purchase motorcycles. Large orders were despatched to South Africa, Eire, Sweden, India and Holland. Once again it was the M-type side valve that was chiefly in demand. When the war did break out in September 1939, the Government requisitioned every model on the Small Heath production line and immediately placed an order for 8,000 M20s. After the fall of France, all the motorcycles that had been taken across the English channel with the BEF were destined to perish upon the beaches of Dunkirk, so to re-equip the armed forces quickly, all production was concentrated on the M20. Many pre-war civilian M20s were rounded up and pressed into service, to suffer the fate of being stood up against the depot wall and shot at with a spray gun loaded with khaki-green paint!

Even the experts at BSA would have acknowledged that the M20 wasn't the most ideal of machines for battlefield service. It was relatively heavy and cumbersome and the low ground clearance could be a hindrance. But reliable it most certainly was, the BSA Competitions Department having seen to that. The decisive factor was that the M20, by its own sheer simplicity, could be

built quickly in the huge quantities now required urgently, and it was that which mattered most. During the first few months of the war BSA built some 350cc ohv prototypes that had the beefy M-type bottom end assembly and after completing successful trials, the Army placed an order for 10,000. But before the necessary production planning could be completed the order was amended to the supply of M20s, to avoid any complications with spares and maintenance. For the duration of the second world war, the M20 continued to be produced and output had soared from 500 to 1,000 a week by the end of the conflict, one machine being wheeled off the production line every five minutes. After the world had been torn asunder some 126,334 machines had been supplied by BSA and despatched across the British Empire and Europe.

The khaki green M20 suffered heavy casualties. Hundreds, perhaps thousands, were unceremoniously dumped or buried when a 'tactical withdrawal' was called for, though many were eventually exhumed by the locals so that even today many a veteran WD M20 still provides the basic motorised transport in every city from Tripoli to Rangoon. As for the survivors, they were bundled together and sold to dealers to be given a new lease of life. Some futile attempts were made to de-militarise some of them and the khaki drab disappeared under a coat of hastily-applied black gloss! It took another twenty years before the last M20 was replaced or pensioned-off from Army service.

With the war over, BSA began producing the civilian M20 to more or less the same specification as in 1940. The M21 returned to production in 1946, both models wearing the new winged BSA motif on the fuel tank.

Val Page had left BSA just before the war but during his three very busy years at Small Heath he

and Herbert Perkins had designed an oil-damped telescopic front fork that could be produced by the otherwise redundant gun-barrel drilling machines. The BSA telescopic fork was a sturdy arrangement with a smooth action which underwent only minor modifications throughout its history. The M20 and M21 were fitted with the telescopic fork in 1948, during which time BSA added another model to the M range. Designated the M33 it comprised a newly-developed 85mm x 88mm ohv B33 engine slotted into the M-type chassis. Due to the B33 being derived from the M-type crankcase assembly, the changes to the cycle parts were minimal, in fact, the only difference was that the ohv engine required an oil strainer for the engine delivery line whereas the side valve engines had a star-shaped return line filter fitted in the top of the tank.

The M33 was a supremely good sidecar machine that offered a good turn of speed and excellent fuel economy, remaining in production until 1958. By its very presence it may have contributed to the downfall of its 500cc side valve brother which many continued to associate with the past war.

The immediate post-war days were the only sporting times when an M20 was put into a competitive arena, even though the saga did have its moments of pure humour. With so many ex-servicemen lying idle and waiting for a demob, various trials, scrambles and dirt track events were organized by army units to ease their boredom. The officers and senior NCOs usually creamed off the more flighty Ariel and Matchless ohv jobs, leaving the rest to make do with the WD M20. Some valiant attempts were made to find just a mite more power, and in some cases this amounted to welding a pad of aluminium on top of the piston in an attempt to increase the compression ratio. Another army trick was to rig up a brake fluid drip feed into the silencer which gave off a sweet aroma just like Castrol R. Even if the M20 couldn't go as fast as a 'works' Norton, at least it would smell like one.

There was one young man who took matters more seriously. He contacted Bert Perrigo, the BSA Competitions Chief, and obtained some uprated fork springs. Having shown such enterprise he was offered a vacancy at Small Heath on leaving the army. Eventually he went on to become a Norton, and later, a Gilera works rider. His name was Geoff Duke, probably the most successful racer of the post-war era, and yet his career began with a lowly M20 BSA!

One event that does still stretch the imagination to its limits occurred in January 1960. A team of eight riders aimed an M20 along a quarter mile stretch of sun-drenched beach in Northern Tasmania. Under approved Australian ACU rules and timekeeping, all the riders managed a speed in excess of 100mph. The fastest run by B.W. Chaplin was measured at 103.4mph! Modifications to the engine included a pair of reground 'Gold Star' cams, larger valves, and a special piston to bring the compression ratio up to 6:1. The inlet tract was blanked off, and a new inlet pipe welded into the barrel, just under the valve. A $1^{1}/_{8}$ inch Amal TT carburettor was positioned near the tappet chest, giving an updraught feed into the combustion chamber. The engine, claimed to run to 7000rpm, and was cradled in a B33 rigid frame with clip-on handlebars. Many standard parts were used, the cylinder head, conrod, piston rings and big-end were all straight off-the-shelf M20 components.

There was never any shortage of expert side valve tuners who could add a little more zest to the otherwise ponderous M20. It was possible to make good advantage

of the low reciprocating weight, if only something could be done about the poor thermal efficiency of the combustion chamber.

The Automobile Association changed over to the M21 in the early 1950s. The larger machine was the better tractor unit for lugging heavy box sidecars laden with tools and motorcar parts. By 1953 the entire fleet of AA Road Service Outfits consisted of M21s which remained the mainstay service vehicle throughout the 1950s and early 60s. Each machine would run up approximately 100,000 miles on duty before being driven back to the BSA factory and exchanged for a new one. The AA found the M21 very durable. Many machines completed a full tour of duty without any need to overhaul the crankshaft assembly. On average, 40,000 miles could be expected before a rebore was required. It must also be pointed out that the M21 had to be thoroughly dependable at all times and in all weathers, to be able to assist motorists in trouble.

Attitudes began to change and even the most stubborn of riders were ready to buy an ohv machine, the 350cc ohv model B31 becoming the most successful BSA 4-stroke. When sales figures for the B31 reached an all-time peak in 1955, the M20 was quietly dropped from the catalogue. The M21 clung on for a few more

years, still making the most of the orders being received from the AA. But by the late 1950s the demand for sidecar hauling machines began to wane, with more and more riders defecting to motorcars.

The BMC Mini and its variants was the chief culprit responsible for sweeping motorcycle combinations from the roads and the M21 was the last of its victims. The AA placed their last order with BSA in 1963 after which the retired RSOs made their last journey in AA colours to the BMC Longbridge car manufacturing plant.

In April 1968 the AA staged a farewell parade for the last 15 M21 RSOs. The outfits rode past in tight formation, with their riders' eyes turned right to take the final salute. The era of the side valve had come to an end.

EVOLUTION

During the formative years as the popularity of the M20 and M21 was being established, BSA applied a number of very significant changes, mainly to the engine layout.

In 1938, with only one production year behind it, the M21 was given revised bore and stroke dimensions to make it the long stroke, higher capacity option of the two side valve models. Using the same 82mm bore meant that a common linered cylinder barrel and conrod could be used. The pistons, however, were different, the M21 component having its gudgeon pin higher up the piston skirt. Later that year, a new six spring clutch was fitted, a far narrower unit with only five friction plates (including the clutch drum) carrying fabric inserts. It became a standard fitting on all BSA models of 350cc capacity and upwards.

1939 was the most important year in the development history of the M20 and M21. The engine was extensively redesigned. The timing gear was completely revised with identical inlet and exhaust cams running on fixed spindles pressed into the crankcase and supported at their outer ends by an outrigger plate. This enabled the outer timing cover to be taken off for inspection without disturbing the timing gears. It also allowed room for an extra ball bearing to support the crankshaft on the timing side, whilst on the drive side, the ball and roller bearings were spread apart to produce a very rigid crankshaft assembly. There was a new set of cylinder barrel and head castings too. The head was retained by ten bolts and the cooling fins were angled across the cylinder portion to direct air on to the valve areas. The spark plug was moved to a position over the inlet valve. The number of cylinder barrel locating studs was increased from four to five, the extra stud being provided just inside the tappet chest. The tappet cover was reshaped and had the BSA 'piled arms' trademark cast in. Other changes amounted to a repositioning of the toolbox, the use of a foot-change gearbox and a change of colour scheme from Brunswick green to silver grey. Already the M20 and M21 were looking quite different from their original 1937 counterparts.

The same year saw the introduction of the M20 de-Luxe. It was intended for the gentleman who preferred a fully-equipped machine with more traditional features. It differed from the standard M20 by having a fishtail silencer and rod operated brakes. Some of these now scarce M20 de-luxe models were known to have been supplied with a hand change gearbox, footboards and fully valanced legshields to keep the real diehards happy!

When the War Office deluged the Small Heath works with orders for the WD M20 they specified a number of cost and time saving changes from the existing civilian pattern. Sidecar lugs were omitted from the frame and the original single spring 'Empire Star' type clutch was fitted. In order to reach high production targets very few modifications were allowed to interfere with manufacture, but due to shortages of rubber, plain steel serrated foot-rests became a standard fitting and the handlebar grips were usually covered in canvas.

Some engine parts were also made in alternative and easier to obtain materials. A set of canvas pannier bags and a rather long sidestand prop were also usually fitted and then, of course, there was an all-over coat of khaki-green drab listed by BSA as 'number three gas-proof camouflage'. In reality it varied from a murky greeny-grey to a rich dark olive green, depending upon who mixed it!

For the North African campaign a special version of the WD M20 was developed with a Vokes air filter sitting on the fuel tank, the rear portion of the tank having been cut away to allow for a convoluted air pipe to be routed down to the carburettor. Some of these overseas WD 20's also had a magneto inspection cap and an oil pressure check button in the timing cover. The appropriate camouflage was listed as 'Egyptian Sand'.

Production of the civilian M20 began as soon as the last shots of the war had been fired and the first machines to leave the factory were no more than black and silver-grey painted WD M20s. By 1946, the M21 had rejoined the fold bringing back with it the six spring clutch and reshaped mudguards. Thereafter, development was slow and modifications were applied merely to keep up with the times. The M20 and M21 were the last BSA models to be fitted with the telescopic front fork. When eventually the fork was fitted in 1948, the front down tube frame member had to be pulled back towards the engine to accommodate the extra wheel movement. The speedometer drive was for a brief interim period taken from the rear wheel. A new gearbox appeared in 1950 which amounted to little more than a new outer case with an enclosed declutching mechanism, the speedometer drive being taken from the internals.

Alloy cylinder heads appeared the next year in an effort to cure some of the overheating troubles always associated with side valve engines. 1951 was also the year when plunger sprung frames made a welcome appearance though most of the initial machines so constructed were sent overseas. The rigid frame stayed in production right until the very end.

In 1955, Amal Monobloc carburettors became a standard fitting, but by the end of that year the M20 had ceased production. Colour schemes had moved on to maroon with cream or chrome tank panelling depending upon the availability of chromium. As always, there was a black option for the fuel tank.

The last major changes applied to the M21 and saw the excellent 8 inch diameter front brake supplied in 1956 and discontinuation of the cowled headlamp in 1958. Thereafter, the earlier type headlamp was specified, supported on brackets.

It's well worth giving a mention to the Automobile Association M21 in view of the many examples that found their way into private hands. Along with the War Office, the AA favoured the single spring clutch and there were countless other departures from the standard model too. Heavier gauge spokes and wheel rims with fully valanced mudguards and re-profiled footrests and handlebars were just a few items requested by the AA to improve the patrolman's comfort and enable the M21 RS0 to withstand the rigours of all-day and all-weather duty. The final AA machines were equipped with a radio powered by a crankshaft-mounted alternator, which prompted the use of a new type of clutch that had its own integral rubber cush drive. There was also a very comprehensive glass-fibre fairing that enveloped the engine. The AA M21 was the last big capacity British side valve

motorcycle but was certainly dressed to look every part of the jet age before making a final bow in 1963.

Production changes

The M20 and M21 were shown for the first time at the October 1936 Show, intended for the 1937 season. Apart from the engine capacities, 496cc for the M20 and 595cc for the M21, the two models were similar with separate gearbox pre-unit construction. The specification included girder front forks, a rigid rear end and 7 inch brakes front and back. A parallelogram fishtail silencer and an instrument panel in the fuel tank were also featured. A 7$\frac{1}{2}$in D142F headlamp was fitted. Finish was all over black with a Brunswick green tank and gold striping. Frames were stamped HM19-101, engines HM20-101 and HM21-101.

1938: The M21 bore and stroke was revised from 85mm x 105mm to 82mm x 112mm, giving a new capacity of 591cc. The cylinder barrel carried an austenitic steel liner. A new six spring and five friction plate clutch was fitted. The horn position was moved from the top of the frame down tube to above the front engine mounting plate. Wheel rims were chromed with black centres. The fuel tank was also chromed, with green panels, and a new oblong BSA tank transfer applied. Frame and engine numbers were as 1937

except the key letter was J instead of H.

1939: During mid-season the engines were extensively modified. Changes were:- New timing gear with both cams running on fixed spindles. Cylinder barrels were given an extra fixing stud inside tappet chest. The number of cylinder head bolts was increased from eight to ten. The cooling fins were re-arranged in a V formation and the spark plug was moved to a position above the inlet valve. An additional ball bearing was added to the crankshaft on the timing side whilst the outer drive-side bearings were moved apart. The timing cover and tappet cover were re-shaped and had the BSA letters and the 'piled arms' trade-mark cast in. One-piece valve guides replaced the earlier two-piece type and the crankcase breather was moved up from the output mainshaft boss to below the crankcase mouth. A footchange gearbox was fitted and the clutch sleeve now had a double row of ball bearings instead of a single row. The cylinder head steady was moved from the front to the rear of the head.

The changes to the cycle parts included:- A new toolbox positioned at the rear wheel support and revised oil and fuel tanks. A speedometer now became standard equipment and was positioned on the left-hand side at the top of the forks. A tubular tail pipe was fitted to the silencer. The finish consisted of matt silver panels on a chrome-plated tank lined out in black. The tank transfer was elliptical. The M20 for this year only. had a 20 inch front wheel. Also, for this year only, a de-luxe M20 was offered. It retained the 19 inch front wheel, and had a rod-operated brake. The exhaust silencer had a fishtail end piece. The finish was generally as the other models. Engine and frame numbers were the same as 1938 except the key letter was K instead of J. The engines incorporating the mid-season changes have the letter S included into the number prefix.

1940: A tubular silencer was fitted. The speedometer drive was taken from the left-hand side of the front hub, and a reshaped rear number plate appeared, with the rear lamp centrally positioned. During the year production of the M21 was suspended and the WD M20 was the only motorcycle to be made for the next four years. It was basically a 1940 civilian M20 except that the frame had no sidecar lugs and the clutch reverted to the original single spring, eight plate 'Empire Star' type. The fuel tank did not have an instrument panel. A 6 in MU42 headlamp was fitted. Special fittings included:- black-out mask, sidestand, canvas panniers, plain footrests and an all-over finish in khaki-green. Engines and frames were stamped with the key letter W.

1945: Production of the civilian M20 began again. It was generally a WD type but with an all-black finish, chromed fuel tank and matt silver panels. The toolbox was enlarged, mudguards were unvalanced and a rear carrier was fitted. Engines and frames were stamped XM20-101 onwards.

1946: The M21 returned to production with the same features and finish as the M20. The fuel tanks adopted the winged BSA metal badge. Engines and frames retained the key letter X.

1947: Due to phasing out of WD M20 stocks, the six spring and five plate clutch re-appeared. The frame once more featured integral sidecar lugs. Engine and frame numbers retained the key letter X.

1948: In mid-season telescopic front forks were fitted. The frame front down tube was repositioned. The speedometer was mounted centrally on the forks with the drive taken from the rear wheel. The fuel tank and toolbox were of the type fitted to the B models. The crankcase breather was located at the rear of the outer timing cover. An MU142 headlamp unit was fitted. The engines and

frames were stamped with the key letter Y.

1949: During the year a new four-speed gearbox appeared with enclosed clutch operating mechanism. The speedometer drive was taken from the gearbox. Stronger fork springs were available for sidecar users and the rear wheel was no longer a QD type though taper roller bearings were retained. A SSU700P headlamp unit was fitted. Engines and frames were stamped with the key letter Z.

1950: A new 60 watt M01L Magdyno unit with MCR2 control box replaced the earlier M01 and MCR1 types. The rear number plate was a MT211 type. The frames began at ZM20-7001, engines ZM20-4001 and ZM21-5001.

1951: Aluminium alloy cylinder heads were fitted with a bronze insert for the spark plug. Plunger type frames became optional with a QD rear hub supported on ball bearings. A 480 type rear number plate was fitted. The frames began at ZM20-10001 (rigid) and ZM20S-101 (plunger). Engines began at ZM20-6001 and ZM21-8001.

1952: Cylinder liners were no longer fitted. Dual seats became optional. Due to shortages of chrome the fuel tanks and wheel rims were painted all over. Frames began at ZM20-14001 (rigid) and ZM20S-301 (plunger). Engines began at ZM20-10001 and ZM21-10001.

1953: A cowled headlamp fork shroud was fitted, headlamp type was SS700P/1 with underslung

pilot lamp. A new toolbox was fitted to plunger framed models. A type 525 rear number plate was fitted with combined stop and tail lights and separate reflector. The tanks were painted maroon and for this year only, chrome striped panelling was fitted to the fuel tank sides. Frames were stamped BM20-101 (rigid) BM20S-101 (plunger). Engines were BM20-101 and BM21-101.

1954: Plastic badges with the 'piled arms' device were fitted to the fuel tanks. A RB107 control box was specified. Frames began at BM20-1502 (rigid) BM20S-1192 (plunger). Engines began at BM20-1001 and BM21-1601.

1955: A two-lobe engine shaft cush drive replaced the four-lobe type. A new type SS700P headlamp was fitted without an underslung pilot lamp. The rear number plate was a 564 type. Steering locks were fitted to all models. Monobloc carburettors were standard equipment with new air cleaners. During the year, production of the M20 ceased. Frames began at BM20-4001 (rigid), BM20S-4001 (plunger). Engines began at BM20-2501 and BM21-4501.

1956: A new 8 inch diameter front brake and a slimmer valanced front mudguard was fitted. Tank finish was maroon with cream panels lined in gold. Frames began at BM20-7001 (rigid) and BM20S-8001 (plunger). Engines began at BM21-7501.

1957: The option on chromed tank panels was available.

1958: The cowled headlamp arrangement was discontinued. A SSU700P type headlamp was supported on two brackets. The M21 was available only to special order. Frame numbers began at BM20-10001 (rigid), BM20S-11001 (plunger). Engines began at BM21-11001.

1959: No changes. Frames began at BM20-10313 (rigid), BM20S-12031 (plunger-estimated). Engines began at BM21-12033.

1960: No changes but production of rigid frames ceased during the year. Frames began at BM20-10451 (rigid), BM20S-13100 (plunger). Engines began at BM21-12901.

1961: To meet requirements for the Automobile Association a crankshaft-mounted alternator was fitted with a special clutch incorporating an integral rubber cush drive. Frames began at BM20S-14201. Engines began at BM21-14301. Alternator versions had the inclusion of the letter A.

1962: No changes. Frames began at BM20S-15061. Engines began at BM21-15453.

1963: Production of the M21 ceased during the year. Frames began at BM20S-15159, engines began at BM21 (A)-15588.

Super Profile

SPECIFICATION

Early models

Model	M20	M21
Year of manufacture	1937-45	1937-40
Capacity (cc)	496	595 (1)
Bore x stroke (mm)	82 x 94	85 x 105 (2)
Compression ratio	5:1	5:1
Bhp	13 @ 4200rpm	15 @ 4000rpm
Valve timing (degrees)		
Inlet opens BTDC	10 (3)	10 (3)
Inlet closes ABDC	55	55
Exhaust opens BBDC	60	60
Exhaust closes ATDC	15	15
Ignition timing (in) (piston position BTDC, ignition fully advanced)	$5/16$ (4)	$5/16$ (4)
Valve clearances (in)		
Inlet	0.004 (5)	0.004 (5)
Exhaust	0.006	0.006
Ignition points gap (in)	0.010-0.012	0.010-0.012
Spark plug type	KLG F70 or Lodge C14	KLG F70 or Lodge C14
Spark plug gap (in)	0.015-0.018	0.015-0.018

Clutch type	Single spring & eight (6) friction plates 'Empire Star' type		Single spring & eight (6) friction plates 'Empire Star' type	
Gear ratios	solo	sidecar	solo	sidecar
4th	5.28	5.94	4.75	5.60
3rd	6.95	7.82	6.25	7.30
2nd	10.87	12.20	9.77	11.50
1st	15.76	17.70	14.15	16.60
Sprocket sizes				
Engine	18 (7)		20 (7)	
Clutch	43		43	
Gearbox	19		19	
Rearwheel	42		42	
Chain sizes (in)				
primary	$^1/_2$ x .305 (8) 69 pitches		$^1/_2$ x .305 (8) 69 pitches	
Rear	$^5/_8$ x $^1/_4$ 95 pitches		$^5/_8$ x $^1/_4$ 95 pitches	
Suspension				
Front	girder		girder	
Rear	rigid		rigid	
Tyre sizes (in)				
Front	3.25 x 19 (9)		3.50 x 19	
Rear	3.25 x 19		3.50 x 19	
Brake drum diameter x width (in)				
Front	7 x 1$^3/_8$		7 x 1$^3/_8$	
Rear	7 x 1$^3/_8$		7 x 1$^3/_8$	
Fuel tank capacity	3 gall (imp) (10)		3 gall (imp) (10)	
Oil tank capacity	6 pint (imp) (11)		6 pint (imp) (11)	
Gearbox capacity	1 pint (imp)		1 pint (imp)	
Generator & Ignition	Lucas MO1 Magdyno		Lucas MO1 Magdyno	
Output	40 Watts		40 Watts	
Voltage & polarity	6 volt negative		6 volt negative	
Ignition points gap (in)	0.010-0.012		0.010-0.012	
Wheelbase (in)	54		54	
Ground clearance (in)	4$^5/_8$		4$^5/_8$	
Seat height (in)	28$^1/_2$		28$^1/_2$	
Overall width (in)	28		28	
Dry weight (lb)	369		370	

Super Profile

Notes

1. From 1938, 591cc
2. From 1938, 82mm x 112mm
3. 1939-45, 10°, 60°, 59°, 9°
4. 1938-39, $3/8$ inch, 1940 on, $7/16$ inch
5. 1938, Inlet 0.004 inch, Exhaust, 0.012 inch
    1939-45, Inlet, 0.008 inch, Exhaust, 0.012 inch
6. 1938-40, Civilian models had 6 spring type clutch
7. 16T for sidecar
8. 68 pitches for sidecar
9. 1939 M20 Standard had 3.25 x 20 inch front tyre
10. 1940 $3^1/2$ gall
11. 1938, 4 pints, 1940, 5 pints

Later models

Model	M20	M21
Year of manufacture	1945-55	1946-63
Capacity (cc)	496	591
Bore x stroke (mm)	82 x 94	85 x 112
Compression ratio	4.9:1	5:1
Bhp	13 @ 4200rpm	15 @ 4000rpm
Valve timing (degrees)		
Inlet opens BTDC	25	25
Inlet closes ABDC	65	65
Exhaust opens BBDC	65	65
Exhaust closes ATDC	25	25
Ignition timing (in) (piston position BTDC, ignition fully advanced)	$7/16$	$7/16$
Valve clearances (in)		
Inlet	0.010	0.010
Exhaust	0.012	0.012
Spark plug type		
Cast iron heads	Champion L10	Champion L10
Alloy head	Champion N8	Champion N8
Spark plug gap (in)	0.015-0.018	0.015-0.018
Clutch type	6 spring & 5 (12) friction plates (including clutch drum)	6 spring & 5 friction plates (including clutch drum)

Gear ratios	solo	sidecar	solo	sidecar
4th	5.28	5.94	4.75	5.94
3rd	6.95	7.82	6.25	7.82
2nd	10.87	12.20	9.77	12.20
1st	15.76	17.70	14.15	17.70

Sprocket sizes				
Engine	18 (13)		20 (13)	
Clutch	43		43	
Gearbox	19		19	
Rearwheel	42		42	

Chain sizes (in)		
Primary	$1/2$ x .305	$1/2$ x .305
	69 pitches (14)	69 pitches (14)

Rear	$5/8$ x $1/4$	$5/8$ x $1/4$
	95 pitches (15)	95 pitches (15)

Suspension		
Front	girder (16)	girder (16)
Rear	rigid (17)	rigid (17)

Tyre sizes (in)		
Front	3.25 x 19	3.25 x 19
Rear	3.25 x 19	3.50 x 19

Brake drum diameter x width (in)		
Front	7 x $1^{3}/8$ (18)	7 x $1^{3}/8$ (18)
Rear	7 x $1^{3}/8$ (19)	7 x $1^{3}/8$ (19)

Fuel tank capacity	3 gall (imp)	3 gall (imp)

Oil tank capacity	5 pint (imp)	5 pint (imp)

Gearbox capacity	1 pint (imp)	1 pint (imp)

Telescopic front fork capacity	$1/4$ pint (imp)	$1/4$ pint (imp)

Generator & Ignition	Lucas MO1 Magdyno (20)	Lucas MO1 Magdyno (20)

Output	40 Watts (20)	40 Watts (20)

Voltage & polarity	6 volt negative (21)	6 volt negative (21)

Ignition points gap (in)	0.010-0.012	0.010-0.012

Wheelbase (in)	54	54

Ground clearance (in)	$4^{5}/8$ (22)	$4^{5}/8$ (22)

Seat height (in)	$28^{1}/2$ (23)	$28^{1}/2$ (23)

Overall width (in)	28	28

Dry weight (lb)	369 (24)	370 (24)

Super Profile

Notes

12. 1945-47 and M21 AA version up to 1961 had single spring 'Empire Star' type clutch
13. 16T for sidecar
14. 68 pitches for sidecar. 70 pitches from 1949
15. 97 pitches plunger frames, solo and sidecar
16. 1948 on, telescopic forks
17. Plunger frame option from 1951
18. 7 inch x $1^1/8$ inch telescopic forks. 8 inch x $1^3/8$ inch from 1956
19. 7 inch x $1^1/8$ inch plunger frame
20. MO1L 60 watt Magdyno from 1950
21. Positive earth from 1953
22. $5^1/2$ inch for telescopic fork frames
23. $30^1/2$ inch for telescopic fork frames
24. For plunger and telescopic fork models, weights are, 365lb M20 and 376lb M21

Amal carburettors

Model	Type	Choke size (in)	Main jet	Pilot jet	Throttle slide	Needle jet	Needle position
M20 1937-38	76/014-45A with 64/078 float chamber	1	170	–	6/4	.1065	3
M20 1939-45	76/014-45A with 264/069 float chamber	1	170	–	6/4	.1065	2
WDM20 1939-45	276C/1B	1	170	–	$6/4$	.1065	2
M20 1946-54	276C/1B	1	170	–	6/4	.1065	2
M20 1955	376/21 Monobloc	1	240	30	6/4	.1065	3
M21 1937-38	76/024-51A with 64/078 float chamber	$1.^1/16$	170	–	6/4	.1065	2
M21 1939-40	76/024-51A with 264/069 float chamber	$1.^1/16$	160	–	6/4	.1065	2
M21 1946-54	276/C/1B –51A	$1^1/16$	160	–	6/4	.1065	2
M21 1955-63	376/23 Monobloc	$1^1/16$	250	30	6/4	.1065	2

January 18, 1951. MOTOR CYCLING

Sturdiness with reliability is the keynote of this famous 496 c.c. side-valve B.S.A., for long a popular model with Service and " civvy street " riders alike.

ROAD TEST

AMONGST motorcyclists there is probably no subject so lengthily and learnedly discussed as the evergreen argument, " o.h.v. versus s.v." That the former system of operation is nowadays vastly more popular makes no difference to the vehement loyalty of the side-valvers who, though they may not be so widely catered for by manufacturers, are firmly convinced that their own choice of layout gives them " that little something the others haven't got." Exactly what that something is may not be easy to define, for there is ample proof to-day that an engine with valves in the head can be built to give a performance similar in almost every respect to that of a side-valve, in so far as flexibility and pulling power are concerned, plus even greater economy.

Nevertheless, there *is* something distinctive about a side-valve, and perhaps one of the chief reasons for the preference expressed towards it by so many riders is the comparative simplicity of the power unit, with its accent on top-end accessibility—an invaluable feature when time for routine maintenance is limited.

Robust characteristics do not detract from neatness in the disposition of handlebar equipment. Note the clean tank " lines," the generously dimensioned knee grips and the damper fitted as standard in view of the suitability of the model for sidecar work.

A20

Road Tests of Current Models

The 496 c.c. Side-valve Model M20

B. S. A.

A 1951 Example of a Machine with a Proud War Record and Employing a Type of Engine long Favoured for Flexibility and a Capacity for " Slogging."

Indeed, there are, no doubt, many readers who served with the Forces during the war who will recall that certain side-valve models were held in high esteem in the D.R. sections— for the very good reason that such mounts required so little attention to keep them serviceable. So it was with the 496 c.c. M20 B.S.A., of which type many thousands did yeoman service in military guise, operating satisfactorily in climatic temperatures varying from desert heat to arctic cold.

An Alloy Head

For peace-time work some changes have been made in the specification of the machine that saw such extended war service. Hydraulically damped telescopic front forks replace the former girder units and increase comfort and handleability. An alloy cylinder-head assists the engine to digest Pool petrol without pinking, harsh running or excessive heat. Appearance, too, is much enhanced by a change from dull khaki or olive green to shining black enamel and a chrome-and-silver petrol tank. Gone also is the lamp-mask, restricting light available for night journeys; an 8½-in. Lucas headlamp provides ample light when darkness falls.

As regards performance, although a certain amount of weight was necessary on the kickstarter, a routine was arrived at to ensure easy starting. With ignition half-retarded, and air-lever shut, the engine fired easily after two or three prods with the exhaust valve raised, and it quickly settled down to a slow, even beat. Weather conditions controlled the time required for warming up; on anything but the coldest days the air-lever could be fully opened

(Right) On the road, the tester's outstanding impression was of the machine's sustained capacity for hard work coupled with comfort and good steering.

(Below) An alloy cylinder head is an important feature of the latest post-war M20. The gearbox end-cover and clutch-operating mechanism, too, have been considerably modified.

performance range, it was possible to ride to a standstill with the feet on the rests.

Deliberate movement was necessary if entirely satisfactory gear changes were to be made. The fairly hefty flywheels made themselves felt if rush tactics were employed, and the machine bounded forward if anything so out of character as a racing gearchange were attempted. Carried out with due deliberation, gear selection was quite pleasant and positive, and the pedal possessed a range of movement that was fair compromise between too much and too little. Clutch operation was firm, without being excessively heavy, and the engagement smooth and without slip—smooth enough, coupled with the steam-engine pulling, to make second-gear standing starts easy and snatch-free.

This steady pulling at low engine revs. is expected of any side-valve and the M20 conformed admirably. Top gear could be held until each power stroke could be counted, after which, with the ignition retarded slightly, the mount could be accelerated away without sign of snatch. Early gear changes paid dividends and top gear could be engaged at 30 m.p.h. without serious detriment to performance. This freedom from toe wagging gave added pleasure to normal touring. Except for enforced halts at major roads or traffic lights there was little need to use any gear other than top and, for normal purposes, it is a one-gear machine.

after a few minutes' running and then, with the engine warm, ignored.

The riding position was soon adjusted to personal requirements. The footrests, on their splined hangers, have a wide range of vertical adjustment and the footchange lever of the four-speed gearbox, also mounted on a splined shaft, can be moved in sympathy. The non-adjustable brake pedal could, with advantage, have been set an inch or two lower to bring the lever pad to a more easily operated position. Vertical adjustment is available for the handlebars, and the clip-on controls can be placed within easy reach and at the most comfortable angles.

"Springer" Prospects

At the time of the road test, no spring frame was listed in the specification, but a coil-spring plunger unit will soon be available, if required. In spite of the lack of suspension at the rear, the M20 provided a comfortable ride and there was a noticeable absence of rear-wheel hop on all but the worst type of secondary road. At the front, the B.S.A. telescopic forks did their job in an admirable fashion and the front wheel remained firmly on the ground, following faithfully whatever line the rider desired through bends. This handling, not always expected in a staid, touring machine weighing approximately 370 lb., was a characteristic that ensured a good cruising speed, whilst grazed footrest rubbers indicated the degree to which the machine could be heeled over. At the other end of the

Little change has been made to the lay-out of the near-side of the machine. Here is seen the excellent accessibility of all components likely to require periodic maintenance.

A21

MOTOR CYCLING   *January 18, 1951.*

BRIEF SPECIFICATION OF THE 496 c.c. "M20" B.S.A.

Engine: Single-cylinder s.v.; 82 mm. bore, 94 mm. stroke; 496 c.c.; all valve gear totally enclosed and positively lubricated; heat-treated aluminium-alloy cylinder head; Amal carburetter, type 276C-1B Lucas Magdyno.

Transmission: Primary chain ½ in. by .305 in. running in oil-bath case. Rear ⅝ in. by ¼ in. Four-speed B.S.A. gearbox, ratios 5.28, 6.95, 10.87, and 15.76 to 1; gearbox operated by enclosed positive-stop foot change.

Frame: Cradle type with B.S.A. hydraulically controlled telescopic front forks incorporating hand - controlled steering damper, spring-up rear stand.

Wheels: Chromium-plated rims taking Dunlop 3.25-in. by 19-in. tyres front and rear; 7-in. front and rear brakes.

Tank: Welded steel fuel tank, capacity 3 gallons; built-in knee grips.

Dimensions: Saddle height 30½ ins.; wheel-base 54 ins.; ground clearance 5½ ins.; weight 369 lb.

F.nish: Black enamel with silver and chromium tank.

Equipment: Lucas lighting with 8½-in. head-lamp; electric horn; speedometer.

Price: £118, plus £31 17s. 4d. purchase tax =£149 17s. 4d.

Makers: B.S.A. Cycles Limited. Small Heath, Birmingham, 11.

Main-road hills could be surmounted without the aid of third gear, the engine pulling without protest, and the machine could, if baulked, be accelerated away on the majority of gradients.

A comfortable cruising speed appeared to be midway between 45 and 50 m.p.h., and this gait could be held indefinitely without distress. However, if this top limit was exceeded for any length of time, some discoloration of the exhaust pipe resulted. This was the only sign of stress shown throughout the test and it was virtually impossible to make the power unit protest, however carelessly the throttle was used.

Braking

Entirely adequate brakes, 7-inch front and rear, are fitted and they did their job smoothly and efficiently at any speed within the machine's capabilities. The front unit alone was powerful enough to stop the machine in anything but an emergency, and was pleasant to use. Careless application of the foot brake locked the rear wheel, but clumsiness was mainly responsible when this occurred. Heavy application of both levers produced no indication of one-sided braking and straight-line stops were invariably forthcoming.

Night riding, to the full extent of the machine's capabilities, was made pleasant by the large and efficient Lucas head lamp. Providing a good spread of light, the beam had an excellent range and cruising speed was limited by engine performance rather than by lighting facilities. The dip switch is neatly and conveniently mounted on the handlebar clutch lever and, in the dipped position, the beam gives adequate illumination without annoyance to oncoming traffic.

Vibration was absent throughout the normally used engine speed range, becoming apparent only at maximum throttle openings. With an engine that is designed to pull rather than rev, there is an inherent "feel" that is, perhaps, part of the machine's make up and is in no way objectionable. Certainly this unit was entirely free from any "period."

Petrol consumption at touring speeds of between 45 and 50 m.p.h. can be anticipated to be approximately 70 m.p.g.

and, for leisurely pottering, an appreciable increase on the 30 m.p.h. figure of 82 m.p.g. in the test panel can be expected. Side-valve engines are normally rather uneconomical at wide throttle openings, but in view of the top gear ratio of 5.28 to 1, the M20 was not unduly thirsty.

The engine and exhaust noises were quite inoffensive; the tappets and, when cold, the piston, could be heard, but, once the engine was warmed up, piston noise disappeared. The exhaust note was dull and, even at large throttle openings, never offensive. On small throttle openings in top gear the note was very subdued and, indeed, all but inaudible at cruising speeds.

Emphasis must be placed on the ability of this machine to give trouble-free and unobtrusive service. This is, of course, another side-valve tradition, satisfactorily upheld. Many weeks of use resulted in a mileage that is exceptional by routine road test standards and, after an early readjustment of the exhaust valve lifter, the machine was run without any maintenance whatsoever other than the necessary addition of fuel and oil. It would appear impossible, in a normal road test, to cover a mileage sufficient to test this ability to run without adjustment.

Maintenance

When the need for service does arise the accessibility of the M20 makes all normal maintenance the simplest of jobs. Top overhauls can, of course, be carried out with the petrol tank in place and tappet adjustment is childishly easy. A complete top overhaul could be made without difficulty in two or three hours.

Sensibly mounted on rubber washers, the Smiths 80 m.p.h. speedometer is located on the steering head and is easily visible. The electric horn gives a pleasant warning note and is conveniently operated by a button screwed to the hand brake lever. The rear stand needed some care and effort to operate, but it held the machine firmly.

Generally, the 496 s.v. B.S.A. is an ideal mount for the leisurely individual for whom motorcycling must be a convenient and trouble-free mode of transport, calling for a minimum of attention for the maximum of service, and of this mount one outstanding impression is retained: the M20 is ever willing.

Its makers are B.S.A. Cycles, Ltd., Small Heath, Birmingham, 11.

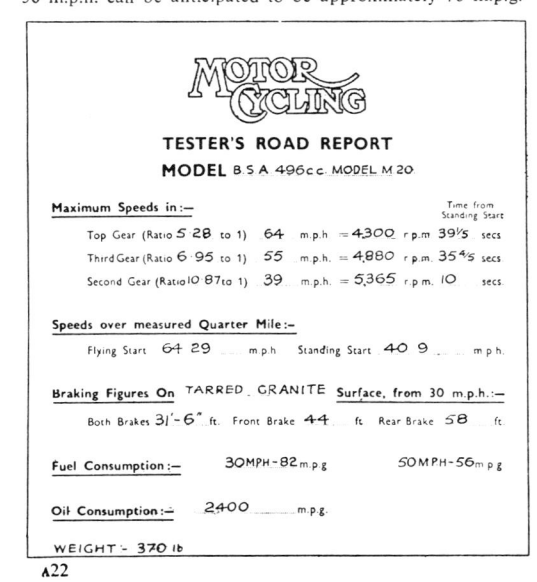

TESTER'S ROAD REPORT

MODEL B.S.A. 496 c.c. MODEL M 20.

Maximum Speeds in :—

			Time from Standing Start
Top Gear (Ratio 5.28 to 1)	64 m.p.h.	= 4,300 r.p.m.	39⅘ secs
Third Gear (Ratio 6.95 to 1)	55 m.p.h.	= 4,880 r.p.m.	35⅘ secs
Second Gear (Ratio 10.87 to 1)	39 m.p.h.	= 5,365 r.p.m.	10 secs

Speeds over measured Quarter Mile :—

Flying Start 64.29 m.p.h. Standing Start 40.9 m.p.h.

Braking Figures On TARRED GRANITE **Surface, from 30 m.p.h. :—**

Both Brakes 31'-6" ft. Front Brake 44 ft. Rear Brake 58 ft.

Fuel Consumption :— 30 M.P.H.—82 m.p.g. 50 M.P.H.—56 m.p.g.

Oil Consumption :— 2400 m.p.g.

WEIGHT - 370 lb.

A22

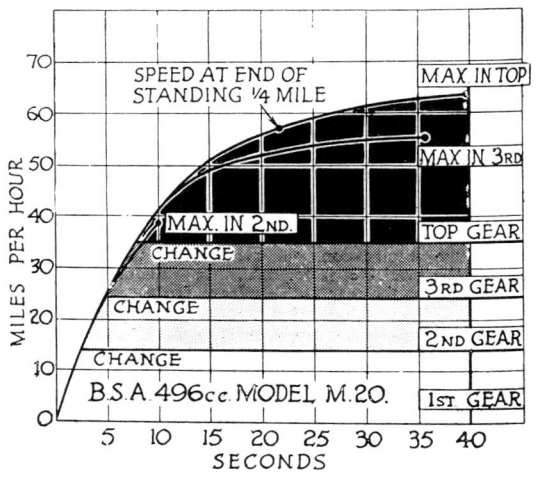

B.S.A. 496 c.c. MODEL M.20.

SPEED AT END OF STANDING ¼ MILE

MAX IN TOP
MAX IN 3RD
MAX IN 2ND
CHANGE
CHANGE
CHANGE
TOP GEAR
3RD GEAR
2ND GEAR
1ST GEAR

MILES PER HOUR.

SECONDS

Super Profile

OWNER'S VIEW

My earliest recollections of the M20 bring back memories of a farmyard hack that had suffered in the hands of a long list of cack-handed amateur mechanics. It said rather a lot for a motorcycle that could keep on running for long periods with hardly any oil in the tank. The engine would still pull up any embankment even though there was no detectable compression and the fuel was more than likely intended for keeping the chicken house warm. The frame had a multitude of fractures held together with overlapping plates brazed or bolted. 'Fine tuning' was achieved by taking off the exhaust pipe and fiddling with the carburettor until the flame sprouting out of the port had less of a pronounced yellow glow. Sadly, the bike that had withstood everything that could be metered out to it died agonisingly at the bottom of a railway cutting. Most of the M-type BSAs I have known have had a hard life and never received anything in the way of routine maintenance, so it is very refreshing to see an M20 or M21 in clean original condition. For anyone brought up on a diet of swinging arm-framed ohv singles or multis, an M20 or M21 presents an alternative style of motorcycling.

I found that the 500cc M20 and 600cc M21 each had their own characteristics. The M20 pulled away smoothly and could cruise ceaselessly over any terrain with little need to make throttle and gear adjustments. Compared to an ohv machine, acceleration was pretty dismal, even overtaking slow lorries required a long view of straight road. Once at speed only the gentle patter of the exhaust could be heard and although vibration could be felt through the handlebars and footrests, it wasn't anything like the high pitched throb experienced from some high revving engines. Town riding was a pleasure, I could change into top gear without any snatch from a speed as low as 15mph.

Whilst sampling a ride on a friend's WD M20 I was surprised to find it so tractable, with no wheelspin even on a muddy field that had been churned up by hundreds of motorcars at a local old vehicle rally. A session on a plunger-framed M21 revealed that the larger engine put out plenty of low speed punch smoothed out by a pair of very hefty flywheels. The full effects of flywheel inertia could be felt when the throttle was backed off.

Starting any of the 'borrowed' machines called for a positive and followed-through kick, otherwise the engine would spit back through the carburettor and send the lever crashing into your ankle. I also found the brakes quite safe and the gear change positive but slow. The M20 wouldn't allow itself to be forced into any changes of speed or direction.

After talking to many owner-riders, a general picture of certain M20/21 rules and habits began to build up. A retired AA Patrolman with half a million M21 miles chalked up recommended changing both the primary and final drive chain split-links every three to four thousand miles. Having to repair a broken primary chain at the roadside involved taking out eighteen small screws before the chaincase cover could be taken off, a tedious job especially when the weather was foul. High grade fuels should be avoided; the low compression engines are quite happy to run on low octane petrol.

Almost without exception, all long-distance voyagers kept a spare exhaust valve and headgasket in the toolbox. The rear right-hand cylinder barrel nut is in an awkward position so if the cylinder barrel does have to be lifted, it's best to have a 3/8 inch spanner in the toolkit with the shank bent at 45 degrees near the head. Correct wheel alignment is important to maintain; the original toolkit included a gauge that located between the rear lower frame member and the wheel rim. Other tools worth having include a valve spring compressor (suitable for a side valve engine), and a magneto pinion extractor. Both types of clutch also require an extractor; the single spring type unit also needs a spring compressor.

For many years the name A.G. Jeal has been well known amongst BSA enthusiasts, especially owner-riders of pre-war models. As the former BSA marque specialist for the VMCC, Gordon has answered letters from all over the world covering problems associated with almost every machine bearing the 'piled arms' badge.

Ever since the late 1940s, Gordon has owned an M21 that has in either solo or sidecar form provided many thousands of enjoyable miles, enabling his family to visit countless places. The same M21, registration number JKN 401, has undergone quite a few changes in all this time but is still regarded as part of the family.

When I visited Gordon at his Coventry home innumerable M20 and M21 documents were at the ready, including a handwritten notebook produced during the war and crammed full of servicing data and general comments about the WD M20.

We had a long and very enjoyable discussion about the BSA side valve singles trading various items from our own collections. Here are Gordon's comments when interviewed on his life and times with the BSA side valvers.

OW: How did you become interested in the M20 and M21?

AGJ: I was introduced to the M20, as so many people were during the war, when I was a vehicle mechanic in the REME. I worked on and rode all the WD types and developed a fondness for the M20. In the notes that I wrote in North Africa in 1943, I recorded my hopes of using one after the war.

OW: When did you actually buy your first M21?

AGJ: Well, after the war I had an Indian V-twin. It suited me very well but a friend wanted it and offered me a swap for his 350cc AJS which was worth considerably more. Later, I wanted a sidecar machine and saw an M21 advertised for sale in a sweet shop window. It had done only 5,000 miles and was attached to a VP 'Viper' sports sidecar mounted on a BSA type 20 chassis. I bought the machine and JKN 401 has been with us ever since. That was in 1948!

OW: What condition was the M21 in and how many miles has it run up?

AGJ: It was in excellent condition when I bought it. A note was once published in *The Compass,* the Sidcup and District MCC's magazine, mentioning that JKN 401 had completed 100,000 miles without a rebore or any new engine bearings being fitted. Eventually the VP sidecar was replaced with a child-adult type and then a piston ring broke up and damaged the piston. I fitted a B31 engine and used the machine in this form for some time. My work took me abroad so the M21 was dismantled and stored under the bench. Some while after my

return to this country it was rebuilt by my son, using parts of the original engine and other units that had been acquired over the years. It provided him with many miles of useful transport over a considerable period. When it came back to me I rebuilt it and fitted a Watsonian 'Monarch' sidecar. For several years it has given us good service as back-up transport to the car and being used in VMCC events and pleasure outings. Currently, it is off the road undergoing another overhaul.

OW: Have you ever experienced difficulty obtaining any spares for it?

AGJ: Over the years I seem to have collected quite a few useful spares so I can't say that I've had any problems. I believe certain mudguards, tanks and other cycle parts can be a little difficult to find.

OW: What sort of performance does the M21 outfit provide?

AGJ: Top speed is 55mph and she'll cruise for ever at 40-45mph. Handling is quite satisfactory and in their day the brakes were very good. However, I'm planning to fit a brake to the sidecar wheel. Fuel consumption is a steady 50mpg.

OW: Is JKN 401 in everyday use? And do you think it is a practical form of transport?

AGJ: Since I retired I use the M21 only for club events and the odd outing. I think that the M21 is a practical machine even today! It has good enough performance and lighting for today's traffic. When I was working and there was a bit of snow and ice about I preferred using the M21, leaving the car at home.

OW: Have you ever won any prizes with the M21?

AGJ: Oh yes! I remember winning the best sidecar cup at a Boxing Day meeting; mind you, I reckon all the BSA riders clubbed together and voted for it en bloc! Apart from that I've picked up a few trinkets and mementoes on my travels, reminders of some very happy days.

OW: Do you ever enter any

sporting events?

AGJ: Yes, Vintage road trials mainly, the annual Coventry to Brighton run is a favourite. I must admit I'm not really interested in concours-type contests.

OW: Have you ever been a member of any motorcycling clubs and do you think that it helps to be a member of a club? Do they have any major events?

AGJ: I honestly can't see how you can ride for so many years and miles without being a member of a club. I've been a member of the VMCC since 1950. I joined the Sidcup and District MCC in 1947 though I left that in 1969 when I moved to the Midlands. Last year I joined the BSA Owners Club – oh – I'm also in the Association of Pioneer Motorcyclists and the Brooklands Society! The amount of technical information obtained from club membership is incredible, not forgetting the many friends made all over the country.

The VMCC have many events of all types throughout the year. The Founders Day rally organised by the VMCC and the annual BSA Owners Club one-day rally are just two of the major events that are certainly worth attending.

OW: Have you found a particular specialist useful in maintaining your M21?

AGJ: If I ever do need anything then Dick Lewis of Lewis and Sons of Weybridge always prove helpful. I've always had a good rapport with him and his stocks of spares are very impressive. I've also heard good reports about Russell Motors of London.

OW: How would you sum up the enjoyment you get from the M21?

AGJ: I have been riding for some fifty years and have enjoyed riding a number of different machines but the M20 and M21 do stand out for the amount of pleasure that they have given.

OW: Finally, what would you say to anyone contemplating buying an M20 or M21?

AGJ: Well, the first advice I'd give to anyone buying an M20 is, please learn how to ride one first! People don't realise that the old side valve machines are entirely different from modern machines. I keep reading articles describing the poor handling of the BSA M20, usually written by people who can't ride or have never ridden an M20. A side valve BSA requires a certain amount of skill and experience if it is to be enjoyed to the full. The ignition control is there to be used and not just left in the fully-advanced position and forgotten. Try to start it without retarding the ignition and you are liable to be hobbling around for a while afterwards.

In contrast to the experienced views of Gordon Jeal I contacted Pete Disson, a younger rider who has recently taken to the roads on an M20 after owning more modern BSAs. Pete caused quite a stir when an article in the BSA Owners Club magazine, *The Star*, told of how he rescued an ex-WDM20 and brought it back home from America. Nowadays both bike and rider are well-known figures at rallies and meetings, especially when Pete is wearing the appropriate world war two despatch rider's gear. Here are his answers to a range of questions about discovering a side valve BSA.

OW: How did you become interested in the BSA M20 and M21 side valve singles?

PD: Initially, it was just curiosity, although from the remarks being made by older riders in the BSAOC I must have been a bit of a masochist to even consider buying one! Perhaps its a mixture of my interests in BSA and British history that led me to buying a WD model.

OW: When did you buy your M20?

PD: I first heard about it in 1980. I was visiting an American friend in San Francisco. He told me about a couple of old single cylinder BSAs that were for sale. There was the M20 and a DBD Gold Star. I bought them both for $800. Actually, it seemed a good idea at

the time and not having ridden any old bikes before I thought it might be rather novel.

OW: What condition was the M20 in?

PD: The bike had been completely stripped down and most of it had been painted in a dark gloss green. Probably because of the climate out there all the parts were in good condition and very few items were missing.

OW: Have you any advice for someone faced with an M20 renovation?

PD: My general advice, which would apply to any renovation, is to do your homework first regarding the original specification. If possible, get hold of a parts book as well as a workshop manual. Also, a very useful reference, particularly on WD M20s, is the Photo Library of the Imperial War Museum.

OW: Did you have any difficulty obtaining any parts?

PD: Yes I did. The correct period rear light is very hard to come by as is the correct horn button. Blackout masks are also a bit rare. Although the throttle twist grip came with a canvas cover, I found it necessary to cut up an old leg gaiter to make a grip for the left-hand side.

OW: What kind of performance and handling does your M20 have?

PD: Considering the tyres are thirty years old, with a very soft Michelin front ribbed type dated 1951, and

a very hard Firestone rear dated 1956, the handling is quite good in the dry. The rear tyre is slippery when wet and slow speed braking causes the front end to wobble. Performance is quite lively when accelerating; I was quite surprised about that! Top speed though seems to be about 50mph with 45mph a very comfortable and easy cruising speed.

OW: Is your WDM20 in regular use? Do you find the running costs high and is it a practical everyday machine?

PD: No, I don't use the bike very often as it's not my only transport. When I am using it though, fuel consumption is very good at approximately 45mpg. I would say that because of the simplicity of the bike it is a very practical everyday machine.

OW: Have you entered any sporting events, concours etc., and won any awards?

PD: The M20 has mainly been used as a display with an army despatch rider figure sitting on it. At the 1984 Bristol Classic Bike Show I was awarded a Highly Commended rosette for the display.

OW: Do you belong to any clubs and do you think it helps?

PD: I belong to the BSA Owners Club and this helps in as much as gaining knowledge of parts suppliers, either trade or private and making contact with other riders who own similar machines.

OW: Is there a particular specialist whom you found useful?

PD: In the south of the country I can't recommend Russell Motors of Battersea highly enough. I've had no cause to search elsewhere for parts. Russells must have the largest stock of new parts in the world for these machines.

OW: How would you sum up the enjoyment you get from your WD M20?

PD: Partly novelty value of course for it's the only rigid-framed machine I have ridden. It's also very comfortable to ride at a comparatively slow speed because it gives you time to enjoy the roads, your riding and the scenery.

OW: What has been the longest journey ever undertaken on your WD M20?

PD: In 1982, I attended the BSAOC International Rally in Holland. Apart from a puncture on the way, the bike went like a dream, with no problems over a round trip of nearly 600 miles.

OW: Do you think there are any particular weaknesses of the M20? Have you ever encountered any problems.

PD: The M20 was designed for rugged use so I don't think there are any particular weaknesses. I have heard that they blow head gaskets and burn out exhaust valves but mine hasn't yet. What I do make sure of is that when using the valve lifter it has fully returned and is not left partially opened. Also, I did have some evaporation problems before I fitted the correct gasket between the carburettor and cylinder head.

BUYING

There can't be many single cylinder British motorcycles easier to obtain and restore than the M20/21 series. It wasn't long ago that a complete M20 could be had by merely asking and Pride and Clarke were selling ex-government reconditioned engines for just a few shillings. Nowadays, of course, even the most decrepit example will involve a little hard earned cash, but by their sheer abundance, finding parts should not present any problems. There was a time recently when pistons for the M21 were hard to come by, which accounted for a lot of owners fitting an M20 engine instead. Thankfully, the demand for M21 pistons has been met, and this gives a good illustration that as long as the M20 and M21 continue to be used on the roads, there will always be a need for new parts to be made.

Some cycle parts such as mudguards, toolboxes and fuel tanks can require a more dilligent search. Owners of pre-war models are isolated from the mainstream of M20/21 riders as the engines built before 1939 are very different and spares must be getting rare.

Even though the general design was extremely rugged, long lasting and unbelievably reliable it was not without its share of troubles. Overheating was the most common malady. The exhaust valve led a hard life and any seasoned M20 rider will recommend taking off the cylinder head every 2000 miles to lap the valve back onto its seat. The overheating problem wasn't purely confined to the BSA, it was all a part of owning a side valve engined motorcycle. More often than not, running hot was due to a lack of appreciation that an old side valve slogger does require skilful use of the manual advance-retard lever and a certain instinct is needed to stoke up a side valve engine properly.

Running on a late spark for a prolonged period produces a noticeable change in the performance of an ohv engine but on a side valve it doesn't, not until one is faced with a burnt-out exhaust valve or a blown head gasket. So, by its very simplicity, the side valve layout does tend to make a rod for its own back. However, numerous yarns about the infallibility of the M20/21 are written down in motorcycling folklore. There was one story that did the rounds some time ago that involved an M20 rider who, through his own neglect, blew the cylinder head clean off and replaced it by wedging a block of wood underneath the frame top tube, where it remained for many thousands of miles! Another favourite source of humour down at the motorcycle club is to witness the exhaust pipe of a tired-out M20 glowing a distinct cherry red in the dark. In the event of a blown head gasket, kitchen foil will provide a useful get-you-home replacement.

The later aluminium alloy cylinder heads did help to dissipate heat but the slightest over-tightening of the spark plug will strip the thread. Overheating in one form or another led to another problem when the early two-piece valve guides distorted and went out of line. BSA corrected this by fitting one-piece guides. Starting a hot engine can be difficult but war-time despatch riders got away with this due to the low-octane and slow atomising fuel that was available.

The later single spring clutch fitted mainly to WD M20s suffered from plate tilt, which caused the clutch to drag and overheat. The army issued a directive to show how four small adjuster screws could be added to the central locking ring to enable the friction plates to be set up true. The single spring clutch was designed to run in dry conditions so it was important to ensure that no oil could get through the cover otherwise clutch slip could occur. It was recommended that every so often the clutch should be dismantled and the friction plates cleaned in petrol.

During the war, the WD M20 suffered fork spring breakages but fortunately this didn't manifest itself with the post-war civilian models.

Provided the oil is changed often and the tank flushed out, the lubrication system should never give any trouble. As a part of routine maintenance it's a good idea to give the oil pressure relief valve ball a gentle tap into its seat otherwise a poorly seated ball valve can allow a by-pass of oil down into the sump and cause a large and nasty pool of oil on the garage floor!

Piston seizures are rare and the beefy crankshaft assembly is very long lasting, and can take a lot of punishment. The engine was noted for its mechanical quietness. Noisy tappets should be inspected for wear and the magneto drive pinion will whine if the incorrect thickness of shims have been fitted between the unit and the crankcase platform.

Girder forks come in for a lot of criticism for giving an inconsistent performance. In many cases this is due to the fact that the linkage system is often neglected. A few strokes of a grease gun now and then can make an awful lot of difference to the machine's handling.

The only other vice to afflict the M range is vibration, but this is a condition common to most single cylinder motorcycles. The electrical equipment, although very basic, suffers most. The voltage control box, usually positioned on top of the rear mudguard, is particularly vulnerable and it is worth considering rigging up some sort of anti-vibration mounting.

When it comes to deciding values, the M20 is one of the cheapest British four-stroke singles to buy. The less numerate M21 can be a little more pricey. All versions have their own following. There is a lot of interest in WD M20s these days. For the last few decades owners have been desperately trying to civilianise them, nowadays it's the complete opposite! A WD M20 in good condition can be one of the most expensive types to buy because of the immense amount of interest that surrounds them. The later M21 is regarded by many as the 'pick of the bunch' thanks to the excellent 8 inch front brake and telescopic forks. Pre-war models can be worth quite a lot, commanding a high rarity value. The 1937-38 types are thin on the ground and with spares so hard to find it leaves these green tank and hand gear change models strictly for the connoisseurs and collectors.

To set about buying a suitable M20 or M21 it's a good idea to scan the weekly motorcycling press or monthly glossy 'classic' magazines to get a general feel for current prices of complete machines and spares. Prices always tend to start out rather high so be ready to haggle and don't jump at the first model you see. Autojumbles are an excellent venue for M20 hunting; don't just search through all the heaps of defunct machinery, ask the trader, he'll more than likely put you on to something. If a 'ready for

restoration' does present itself, make an offer, its a good bet that the trader would sooner go home with the cash rather than the rusty metal!

Auctions are also well worth attending but don't get drawn into the frenzy of over-excited buyers. Sometimes the most humble models can fetch excessive prices due to rash and hurried bids. But then, a BSA M20 or 21 gets a bottom billing and with everyone interested in the more attractive ohv machines, good buys can often be picked up.

It really does pay to be a member of a club. Enthusiasts and fellow club members tend to trade amongst themselves at reasonable rates. A lot of bartering and swapping of spares or even complete machines goes on at club meetings. The club magazine or newsletter is also another good source for wheeling and dealing.

Unlike a car, an unwanted motorcycle doesn't present so much of an eyesore. Many machines finished up buried at the back of some outbuilding or were left semi-dismantled in an attic. Complete machines, long forgotten, will continue to be re-discovered for many years yet. Have a chat with workmates, friends and relations – it's amazing what can turn up within an area of just a few square miles.

Many machines that have been put back on the road recently have been built up from individually-obtained parts. The side valve BSA is probably the only old type motorcycle that one would contemplate buying as a box of bits, knowing that a number of parts are missing, but buying a dismantled machine can be very deceptive too, even if the design was simple. It is quite surprising just how many components make up a complete machine.

When inspecting an intended purchase, have a close look at the frame. Many M-type BSA's will probably, at some time in their history, have hauled a sidecar and whereas engines can be rebuilt easily, bent frames can be very difficult and costly to repair.

Before rebuilding or renovating you have to decide how far the restoration is to go in achieving original condition. The so called 'as factory' specification is difficult to define. Although BSA had a reputation for excellent and consistent quality, many time saving and cost cutting methods were employed to reach the weekly output quotas, so anomalies in fittings, equipment and colour finishes did occur. In the immediate post-war years a lot of surplus war production stock had to be used up, which accounts for the late change-over to telescopic forks. With the passing of so many years it's rather a surprise to find a machine still with its original engine. In the heyday of the side valve it was easier to buy a secondhand or reconditioned engine rather than repair the existing unit, even if the problem amounted to no more than a routine rebore.

The M20 and M21 is the one large capacity BSA machine that is least likely to be restored to an absolute original condition or bulled-up for a concours d'elegance. Most riders prefer to just lump together a basic machine, neglecting the niceties of correct cable runs, plated pipes and fittings. It's more important to get the bike on the road and sample a good old reliable BSA side valve single.

CLUBS, SPECIALISTS & BOOKS

Clubs

Although there is no club specifically for M20 and M21 singles, owners have the choice of joining any of the following clubs to take full advantage of the services they provide.

The **BSA Owners Club** has countless rider-enthusiasts amongst its ranks and any event held by the BSAOC is almost certain to have an M-type model in attendance. The BSAOC has over thirty branches throughout the UK, with many overseas associated clubs and branches. A full social programme is organised with arranged meetings up and down the country. The club offers a range of services including an M20/M21 model specialist, a librarian and a spares information consultant. Each member receives a monthly magazine, *The Star* and a services handbook. The BSAOC can also provide data on machine identification for registration dating. For full details contact:-

Alistair Fitzgerald
12 Plant Lane
Long Eaton
Nottingham
England

The **Vintage Motor Cycle Club** also organises a vast array of events for its yearly calendar and provides a full compliment of services. All models that are 25 years old or more are eligible for VMCC membership. For full details, contact:-

Jim Hammant
'Red Oaks'
Mill Lane
Lower Shiplake
Henley-on-Thames
Oxon
RG9 3LN
England

Owners of WD M20s may be interested in joining the **National 39-45 Military Vehicle Club.** This club caters for all types of Second World War military hardware and the BSA M20 is certainly welcomed to complete the convoy! Many of its members are interested in historical research and even dress up in the appropriate WW2 uniform. The National 39-45 club has also supported the film industry in re-enacting battles. For further information contact:-

Mick Peters
19 Preston CLose
Stanton-Under-Bardon
Leicestershire
LE6 0XT
England
Tel. Markfield 243610

Specialists

Reading the popular motorcycling newspapers and magazines will provide names and addresses of individuals and companies that specialise in BSA M20/M21 spares. The magazine *Classic Bike* and *The Classic Motor Cycle* will prove very useful. Here are just a few leading specialists who will supply spares and literature.

Russell Motors
125/127 Falcon Road,
Clapham Junction
Battersea
London SW11 2PE.
England
Tel: 01-228 1717
'Russells' have immense stocks of new and secondhand M20/M21 spares.

Lewis and Sons (Weybridge) Ltd
51 Church Street
Weybridge
Surrey
England
Tel: 0932 42210

Have excellent stocks of genuine BSA spares. Lewis's can also provide photo-copied BSA catalogues and other prints.

Bri-Tie Motorcycles
1 Armstrong Street
Swindon
Wilts
England
Tel: 0793 31518

Bri-Tie can supply new gaskets, valves, pistons etc. They also have good restoration facilities such as stove enamelling and chroming. Books and photocopied parts manuals can be provided.

C & D Autos
1193-1199 Warwick Road
Acocks Green
Birmingham B27 6BY
England
Tel: 021-706 2902

Have excellent supplies of post-war BSA spares

Anglo-Moto
Unit 9
Park Lane Industrial Estate
Kidderminster
Worcs DY11 6TT
England
Tel: 0562 742559

Specialise in all 'pre-unit' spares. Worth trying for those 'hard to get' parts.

The following specialists always have plenty of secondhand parts in stock:

RJ Motorcycles
18-20 Hotel Street
Coalville
Leicester
England
Tel: 0530 33297

A. Gagg and Sons
106 Alfreton Road
Nottingham
England
Tel: 0602 786288

Trevs Motorcycles
Unit 11
Rands Lane
Armthorpe
Doncaster
South Yorks
England
Tel: 0302 834343

For exhaust systems, saddles, electrical parts and fittings etc., try:-

Armour Motor Products
784 Wimbourne Road
Bournemouth
Hants
England
Tel: 0384 55151

Books

Here is a summary of books that cover the BSA M20 and M21 side valve singles:

Original BSA workshop manuals and owners handbooks.

Genuine or reprinted BSA publications may be purchased from the specialists listed previously. Copies can also be obtained through membership of the BSAOC or VMCC. Good quality Xerox copies are usually available from Bruce Main-Smith Retail, P.O. Box 20, Leatherhead, Surrey, England. Tel: 0372 375615. BMS are also suppliers of a very useful book entitled **BSA Motorcycles 1935-40**. It's full of facts and detailed information about pre-war M20/M21 models and a special section for WD M20s is included. Two other BMS publications include captioned photographs:- **The First Classic BSA Scene** and **The First Military Machine Scene.**

The Book of the BSA by W.C. Haycraft. Published by Pitmans. This title ran to numerous editions but are all out-of-print. The later editions have good servicing information and they are often found at auctions and autojumbles.

BSA Motorcycles by D.W. Munro. Published by C. Arthur Pearson Ltd. The author was a former Chief Engineer at BSA. Published in several editions and reprints but is now out-of-print.

BSA Gold Star and Other Singles by Roy Bacon. In print and published by Osprey Publishing Ltd., 12-14 Long Acre, London, WC9E 9LB, England. It contains a full history of the M-type BSAs with detailed specifications and colour schemes supported by some excellent photographs.

British Motorcycles from 1950: Vol 2, by Steve Wilson. In print and published by Patrick Stephens Ltd, Denington Estate, Wellingborough, Northants, NN8 2QD Tel: 0933 72700. Volume 2 consists almost entirely of BSA motorcycles. Contains an in-depth study of the Birmingham Small Arms Company from the glorious 1950s to the fateful collapse of 1973. A fully detailed account of the M20 and M21 models is given, with a useful section on production changes, specifications and engine and frame number listings.

The Story of BSA Motorcycles by Bob Holliday. In print and published by Patrick Stephens Ltd, address and phone number as above. A full history of BSA motorcycles with many references and photos of the M20/M21 models.

The Giants of Small Heath by Barry Ryerson. In print and published by Haynes Publishing Group, Sparkford, Yeovil, Somerset, BA22 7JJ, England. Tel: 0963 40635. Although basically a motorcycling book it gives the complete story of the BSA Company, building up to its fall, the reasons why, and the personalities involved. It contains photos and references to the M-type BSAs.

BSA Pre-Unit Singles Owners Workshop Manual by Mansur Darlington. Available from the Haynes Publishing Group, address and phone number as above. Comprises a step-by-step guide to overhauling a BSA single, with photographs and line drawings. Covers the M-type models as well as the 'B' series.

PHOTO GALLERY

1. Over a quarter of the machines supplied to the British Army during World War 2 were BSA M20s. At the peak of production one machine was leaving the production line every 5 minutes. BSA could rightfully claim that 'One in four is a BSA'. This particular machine was built in 1943.

2. WDM20s have their own enthusiasts who lovingly restore them back to wartime specification. In the name of originality riders have to put up with no footrest rubbers, canvas handlebar grips and a blackout mask!

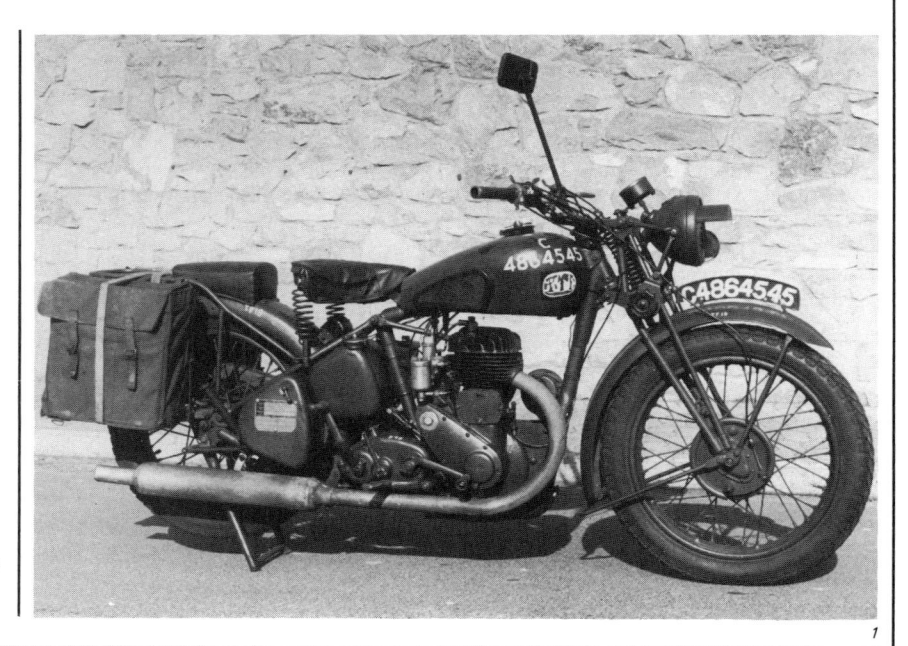

1

2

3

4

5

3. The 496cc engine has a bore and stroke of 82mm x 94mm with a compression ratio of only 5:1. The cylinder has an austenitic steel liner to take two rebores of +^{1}/2mm and +1mm. A rebore should be given when cylinder wear exceeds .010in. The cylinder liner can be replaced but requires some grinding at the base to give the connecting rod adequate working clearance.

4. The carburettor is an Amal type 276 with bottom feed to the float chamber. Many restorers erroneously polish the copper feed pipe; in fact, BSA always nickel plated copper pipes on all their machines. The tank has twin fuel taps, one to act as reserve.

5. The sidestand prop has a hinged bracket clamped to the frame. When not in use it is held by a clip at the rear hub. The footrest rod penetrates through the primary chaincase; a spacer and fibre washer inside the cover forms an oiltight seal.

6. It's quite common to find an Army service plate riveted to the toolbox. It gives information regarding overhaul and servicing by Army Transport units. The registration number 35 YD 34 was from a system adopted during the early 1950s. The small ball-ended fastening knob appeared for many years after the war had ended.

6

7

8

7. The fork mechanism is bristling with grease nipples to lubricate the various bushes and links. The fork spring is located onto scrolls, top and bottom. Removal of the spring requires the front wheel to be supported off the ground.

8. From 1940 to 1948 the Smith's speedometer drive was taken from the front wheel hub as shown here. The gearbox is located onto two slots in the hub shell and must be released before the front wheel can be removed.

9. The primary chaincase cover is retained by 18 cheese head screws. Removal of the cover will reveal a four lobe sprung cush drive and a single spring 8 friction plate clutch unit. The plain inspection cap is a later type BSA fitting; the original had a hexagonal head similar to the magneto cap shown elsewhere. The lug just visible underneath the tank was to hold a tyre inflator, a standard piece of equipment.

10. Rider's eye view of the instruments and switches. The DU42 headlamp has a 6in aperture with the switch and ammeter mounted into the shell. The switch has 4 positions, Off, Tail lamp only (for convoy duty), Low or pilot lamp and High or main headlamp. Many later-built WDM20s had a separate switch panel and no ammeter.

9

10

11

12

13

11. The 5 pint oil tank has the correct butterfly filler cap. The oil feed and return pipes can be seen. The innermost pipe is the feed to the pump, the outer forms the return line from the scavenge stage of the pump. The voltage regulator box is bolted onto the rear mudguard through rubber mounts.

12. Adjustable taper roller bearings support the 7in. diameter brake hub. Although the wheel spindle is fixed, the fork ends are slotted to enable the wheel to be dropped down. The brake backplate is secured to a bridge piece between the fork tubes.

13. The friction damper has an adjustable knob. Regular checks should be made for forklink sideplay with the friction damper loose. The forward lug with brake cable passing through is a relic from pre-war days when some models had dual rod-operated brakes.

14. Many WD20s were specified to have a full set of canvas pannier bags usually mounted in a steel tray. The fire extinguisher is certainly a very useful accessory!

14

15. Rear chain adjustment is achieved with a drawbolt on the right hand side and a snail cam on the left or sprocket side. The large central nut is first removed before the rear hub and knock-out spindle can be detached. The overcentre spring is for the rear stand.

16. This type of rubber kneegrip with diamond pattern was common on most BSA models throughout the 1930s and post-war era. The fuel tank has tapped bosses for the fastening screws.

17. The Lucas M01 Magdyno unit is bolted down onto a platform behind the cylinder. A 40 watt E3HM generator is held onto the magneto with a strap. The magneto points cover is held by a spring clip. The dynamo generator brush gear cover is located with a central screw.

18. Short tubes with flattened ends form the headlamp support through a side socket fixing. Blackout masks are becoming more difficult to find. Although the main bulb has twin filaments, only one was connected and a dip switch was not provided. The bulb could, of course, be turned around in the event of a failure.

15

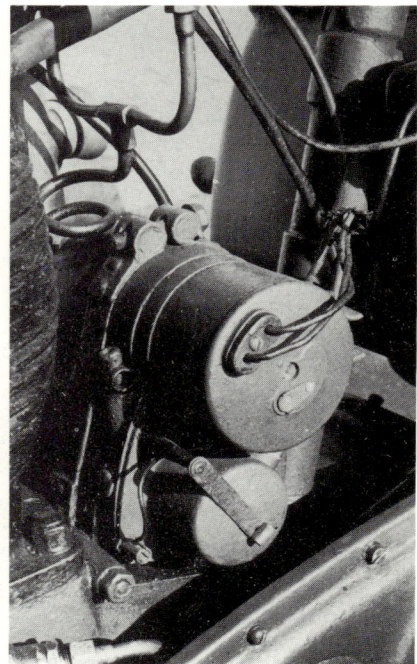

17

16

18

19. The right hand handlebar has a Bowden air lever mounted onto the combination front brake lever. Various makes of handlebar controls were fitted including Amal and BSA pattern types. The dipper switch has been added since the passing of the dismal blackout regulations.

20. The rod-operated rear brake is quite effective though the chainguard was there more to protect the rider than the chain. Chain life was generally good even though it was fairly well exposed to dust, dirt and sand.

21. The earlier type of 4-speed gearbox has an exposed clutch operating mechanism, and was used up to 1948. The kickstart lever is fastened with a cotter pin whilst the gearlever is located on a serrated shaft and locked with a pinch bolt. In post-war times the MOD had a numbering system to designate oil types hence the 545 characters painted on the outer case.

19

20

21

22. *Rider comfort comes courtesy of a Terrys type S707 sprung saddle. A Lycett type was also fitted.*

23. *The majority of WDM20s had a pillion pad bolted to the mudguard. The shape and size of the pad could vary.*

24. *When the War Department ordered machines in batches, each machine was given a serial number. The tank insignia shown here was for 'The Sherwood Foresters'. Army insignia can be displayed provided the said regiment or unit is not in existence. In addition to Army tank motifs there was usually a pair of elliptical transfers bearing the initials BSA affixed to the top flanks of the tank.*

25. *The crankcase pressure relief valve or 'breather' is an important and often overlooked device. It consists of a fibre disc that shuttles back and forth inside a gland body. The crankshaft gases are emitted from the end of a short length of copper pipe.*

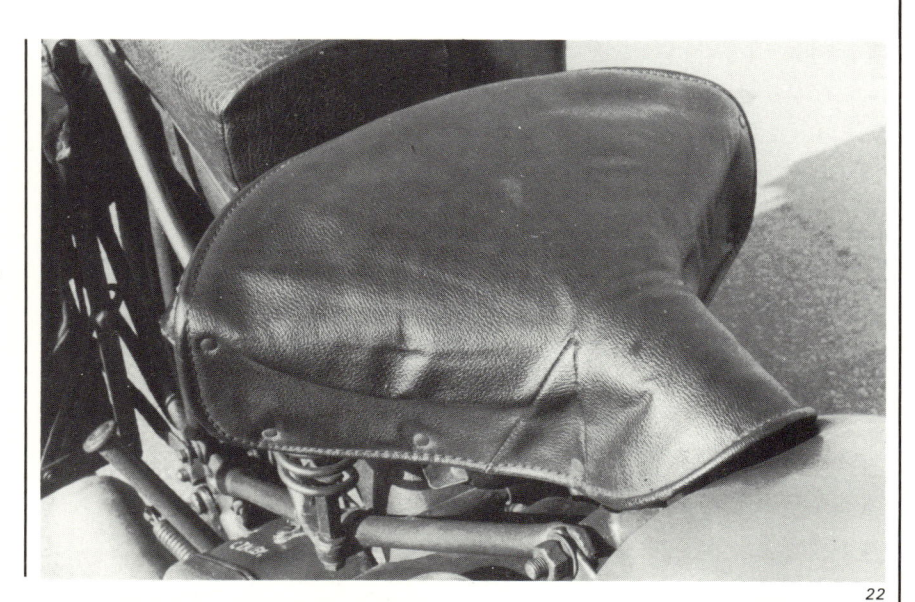

22

23

24

25

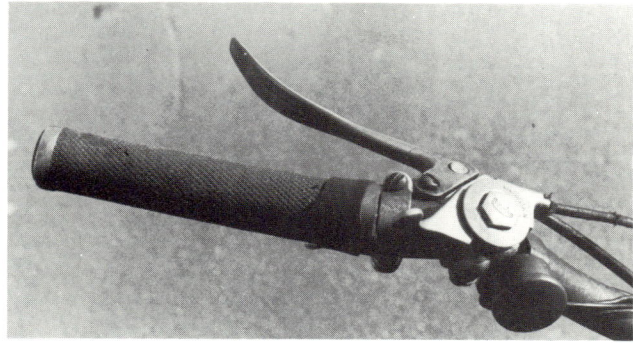

26

26. The canvas handlebar grip obscures a small decompression lever. The combination lever consists of an ignition advance-retard control mounted onto the clutch lever.

27

27. One of the benefits of a WDM20 was this excellent guard plate that protects the otherwise vulnerable oil pump and crankcase.

28. A Lucas RU7E or PUW7E battery was originally specified. The battery is housed in a hinged carrier. The old type lead-acid batteries were very robust and lasted a long time.

28

29

30

31

29. The fuel tank has been truncated near the seat nose. It was to allow for a convoluted air intake pipe running from a tank-mounted Vokes filter. Models fitted with this component were chiefly for North African operations.

30. The hexagonal-headed cap will enable adjustment of the steering head ball races once the pinch bolt has been slackened. The steering head bearings consist of a total of 40^{1}/$_{4}$in. diameter steel balls.

31. A Smith's chronometric speedometer is mounted on a strip bracket. The ammeter (if fitted) would have been a Lucas CZ27 type.

32. This general view shows the bolted-up construction of the frame members and engine plates. An important part of any service is to check all bolts for tightness. Performance of the M20 was rated at 13 bhp with a maximum torque of 220lb/in. being delivered at 3250 rpm.

32

33

34

33. The BSA M20 has a wonderfully mellow exhaust note produced by that long silencer. On WD models the silencer should be slightly upswept. Now on most machines, the lower front mudguard stay has a section of larger diameter tubing. Speculation persists as to the reason for this but it may have been for supporting a .303 Lee Enfield rifle holder, a practice that was soon abandoned.

34. BSA used the very best valve materials; a good job too, some will say! The valve head diameters are 1.737in. inlet and 1.612in. exhaust. The stem diameters are both .346in. A KLG F70 sparkplug was specified, and the KLG plug cap has a knurled Bakelite knob. Perhaps the HT cable should have a little more slack.

35. Certainly in post-war times a fire extinguisher was carried as standard. The Union Jack badges are a recent addition. During the war a single tail lamp was positioned on the mudguard. The number plate and offset lamp are period items and do not look out of place.

35

36. The gearbox oil filler is located at the rear of the gearbox. Just below, but obscured by the exhaust pipe is the drawbolt for adjusting the primary chain. The outer timing cover has a circular projection with the BSA initials cast into it. At the base of the cover a hexagonal-headed screw locates the oil pressure relief ball valve.

37. The Lucas 'Altette' 6 volt horn should have screw type terminals. Many contemporary photographs of the WDM20 show the horn to be located on top of the rear chain-guard.

38. Final versions of the M21 in pristine condition are extremely difficult to find! The 1959 model shown here displays some of the hallmarks of everyday use. In their heyday, M-type BSAs were unlikely to have been lavished with meticulous attention!

39

40

39. The M21 was designed in the days when public roads were still littered with horseshoe nails and frequent punctures were to be expected! The rear hub is located on a serrated boss with a knock-out wheel spindle. BSA's famous 'crinkle hub' was one of the best ever QD arrangements. The rear mudguard has a hinged portion to assist wheel removal. The front wheel is a QD type too and the lower front mudguard stay also acts as a front stand once the wheel has been taken out.

40. Engine numbers were stamped at the drive side crankcase mouth. The number shown here is for a 1959 engine. The raised characters 66-133 are the BSA part number for the cylinder barrel casting.

41. On the later type gearbox first fitted in 1948 the speedometer drive came out from the top just below the oil tank. The problem was overcome by building in a tunnel through the oil tank! The central cap gives access to the clutch operating mechanism and for oil filling.

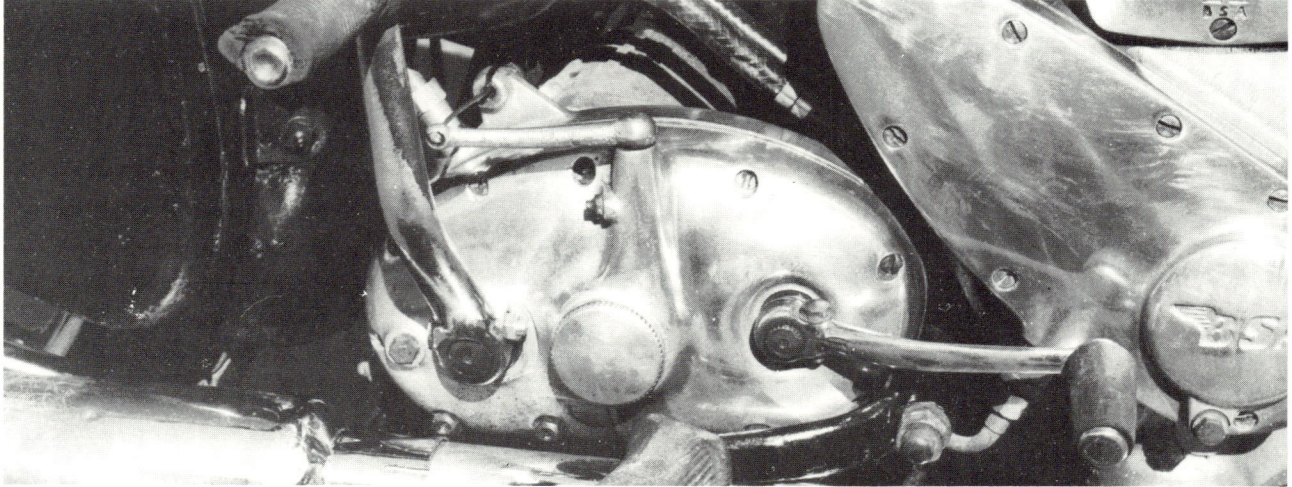

41

42

43

44

42. Unlike other large capacity BSA models the M21 did not receive a nacelle type headlamp in late 1957. Instead, the M21 reverted to a simple side bracket arrangement. The steering lock appeared in 1955 and the steering damper proved to be very useful especially with sidecar users.

43. The owner of this M21 had problems with a warped alloy cylinder head hence an earlier cast iron type has been fitted. The cylinder head steady tube can be seen running back to the frame.

44. BSA adopted their winged B motif in 1946. Rubber knee grips of this pattern with a knurled surface began to appear during the early 1950s.

45. A lifting handle was listed for the plunger-framed models and it was very useful too for hauling the heavy machine onto its centre stand.

45

47

48

46

46. A Lucas 564 rear stop lamp and number plate was fitted from 1956. The rear mudguard hinge can be seen also.

47. The 8in. diameter half width hub front brake was one of the best that ever appeared on a BSA; it was still featured on the A50/A65 unit twins in the mid 1960s. The wheel spindle can be unscrewed with a tommy-bar and withdrawn. The torque arm link is fixed to the alloy backplate and the lower fork stanchion.

48. The speedometer was mounted through some rubber bushes onto the top fork yoke on models built from 1958. Numerous type speedos were specified depending upon the intended type of work and gearing. A mileage recorder or odometer was included, the return to zero knob can be seen. Some M21s even had a 120mph clockface!

49. The long and graceful lever is the ignition advance-retard control. Movement of the lever towards the rider will retard the spark. On some earlier models it was the reverse procedure. The headlamp dipper switch is a Lucas 31563D with combined horn push button.

49

51

50. The 3 gallon fuel tank is bolted to the frame through four lugs. A single fuel tap is fitted on the left side and the tank wells are connected at the front by a short run of copper pipe looping underneath the frame top tube which meant that tank removal was no easy matter.

51. Cylinder barrels made after 1951 did not carry a liner. The M-type side valve engine was very durable and at least 40,000 miles could be expected before a rebore was necessary.

52. The right hand handlebar carried a combination front brake and air control lever. The throttle control is a type 366 with a cable mid-adjuster.

50

52

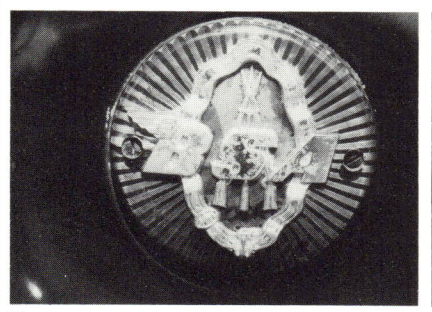

53. The famous BSA 'piled arms' badge had won a reputation for reliability all over the world. A foam rubber backing piece prevents the plastic badge from cracking. 'Piled arms' transfers were applied to the toolbox and steering head-stock. On models built from 1958 the upper lettering should state 'BSA Motorcycles Ltd'; before 1958 it would have stated 'BSA Cycles Ltd'. Also, beware of the fake and gaudy red and bright yellow transfers that have flooded the spares market; the correct type now becoming available should have a cream centre with a lilac-pink belt surround.

54. The lozenge-shaped tappet cover has the BSA trademark cast in. The decompressor lever can be seen on the right. One of the cylinder flange fixing studs is located inside the tappet chest.

55. An Amal 376 Monobloc carburettor was fitted to the M21 from 1955. The alloy spacer forms a long inlet tract. A thick fibre gasket insulates the spacer from the cylinder head and the carburettor has a paper gasket at the flange. The assembly is located onto two studs screwed into the head.

53

54

55

56

57

56. The M21 from 1956 with plunger frame and a very good 8in diameter front brake. It remained virtually unaltered until 1963. Note the round piled arms badge first fitted in 1954.

57. 1953 side valve BSAs had this large striped panel adorning the fuel tank. It's very difficult to tell M20 and M21 types apart, they both used the same cylinder barrel and head castings and all the cycle parts were generally identical.

58

59

58. From 1938 to 1963 a BSA side valve single powered the Automobile Association Road Service Outfits that brought salvation to so many motorists. Here a batch of 1960 M21 outfits are lined up for inspection. Development of the RSO reached a peak with glass-fibre bodied sidecars and on-board radio.

59. The AA RSO lives on! Bob Davis of Livingstone has cherished these two M21 outfits for many years. Both machines have together covered over half a million miles. Bob has been given special dispensation by the AA to display the AA decals at vehicle shows.

60. Somewhere in England, 1941, a troop of despatch riders, all mounted on BSA WDM20s, negotiate a ford. (The Trustees of the Imperial War Museum, London.)

61. DRs await orders. The BSA WDM20 played a prominent part in maintaining a vital communication service throughout the second World War. (The Trustees of the Imperial War Museum, London.)

C1

C2

C1. This splendid WDM20 is owned by Bert Smith of Easton, Nr Wells, Somerset. The BSA M20 was the definitive British motorcycle with separate engine and gearbox construction, cast iron cylinder and head, girder forks and a bolted-together frame.

C2. The WDM20 was based on the 1940 civilian model but with an eight plate 'Empire Star' type clutch, a plain fuel tank with no instrument panel recess and the deletion of sidecar lugs.

C3

C3. The handlebar mirror is there because of 1980s traffic, otherwise the scene could be from the 1940s! It's just as well that the exhaust pipe has 'been in action', a chrome plated exhaust would look out of place. The original system would have been matt silver. The front number plate bearing the machine serial number is a personal addition.

C4. There was no single 'standard' specification that covered all WDM20 machines. They were ordered in batches by the Army and the specified arrangement of fittings and equipment varied from contract to contract. The khaki green finish does have a certain charm! Sometimes even the entire engine received a thick coat of paint. The colour could be anything from a weak grey-green to a deep olive green.

C4

C5

C6

C5. This machine is presented 'fully equipped' with black-out mask, pillion seat, canvas panniers and a fire extinguisher. Both a rear wheel stand and sidestand prop were provided. An inflator was fitted under the fuel tank on the left-hand side.

C6. Here the sidestand prop is brought into action, a very useful device for parking on soft ground. In service, only $4^5/8$in. of ground clearance could pose a few problems and the rear chain was well exposed to the elements but apart from occasional overheating troubles the M20 was very reliable and coped with the most demanding of conditions and riders.

C7. The engine unit had all the hallmarks of Val Page's classic design. The gracefully curving outer timing cover is typical of his style and gives the BSA engine its own distinctive signature.

C8. Note the blunt and slightly concave shape of the forward edge of the gearbox. It dates back to the 'Blue Star' models of the early 1930s, when the casing was matched to the old wet-sump type crankcase. The declutching lever sometimes had a rubber cover to protect the pivot mechanism. The primary chain is adjusted by pulling the gearbox backwards with a draw bolt.

C9. A magneto inspection cap is provided in the outer timing cover. It was usually found on machines destined for service in North Africa or the Far East. It enabled timing checks to be made without the risk of getting sand particles into the timing gear. The tappet cover does not have the BSA 'piled arms' trademark cast into it, unlike post-war civilian machines. The exhaust valve lifter or decompressor can be seen on the right-hand side of the tappet chest; it was provided on every M20 and M21.

C7

C9

C8

C10

C11

C10. The cast-iron cylinder head is held down with 10 bolts and the fins run across the valve area in a vee formation. A thick coat of black paint helps to dissipate heat. One of the cylinder barrel fins has been broken off. The army manual specified that no more than two square inches of cooling fin should be missing – they had a rule for everything!

C11. The M20 and M21 engines were extensively redesigned during 1939. Before, the spark plug was positioned centrally between the valves and the fins all ran parallel, front to back, with the cylinder head held down by only 8 bolts. The redesigned arrangement provided more frontal area for the exhaust port. Note the gap in the cylinder fins just above the tappet cover; this allowed a flow of air to cool the valve stems.

C12. The fuel tank held 3 gallons, giving a range of approx 160 miles. It was bolted to the frame at the front and rear. Twin fuel taps were provided, one acting as reserve. The butterfly type filler cap was a standard fitting.

C12

C13

C14

C13. 'Every feature of the machine typifies rugged simplicity and extreme reliability with economy.' This is how BSA summed up the M21 in their catalogues and advertisements. This 1959 plunger-framed version is owned by Steve Dickens of Plymouth.

C14. During the late 1950s the M21 was intended for commercial and sidecar use, hence it was rare to see the 591cc side valve in solo form. Colour and finish for the M21 hardly changed after 1954. The fuel tank was either maroon or black with cream side panels, chrome plated panels were an optional extra. Frame, forks, mudguards and toolbox etc were black.

C15

C16

C17

C15. During late 1957, the M21 reverted to having the headlamp unit supported on brackets after the headlamp cowl/forkshroud had been dispensed with. Half-width hubs were retained and a rigid frame was still obtainable.

C16. On frames with telescopic forks, the front down tube of the frame is angled back more sharply to join up with the front engine mounting plates. The primary chaincase cover is held in place by 18 small screws making removal a very tedious exercise, especially if a sidecar is fitted!

C17. This particular gearbox appeared during 1949. Removal of the round cap allows for the declutching mechanism to be adjusted and for oil replenishment. The speedometer drive is taken from the gearbox. Accessibility for making adjustments and general servicing on the M20/M21 models is good and only a few tools are required to carry out routine maintenance.

C18

C19

C20

C18. From 1951 alloy cylinder heads were fitted. The finning pattern was the same as the earlier cast iron head fitted to this machine. Many riders favoured the cast iron version, finding it better for suppressing engine noise. The alloy head gained a reputation for having a spark plug thread that was easily stripped.

C19. The round plastic 'piled arms' badge appeared in 1954. The one shown here has an orange appearance through years of basking in the sunshine. BSA adopted the 'winged B' and block letters in 1946 to herald a new post-war era. Ex-Automobile Association type M21s had a plain fuel tank with no badge recess. Many of these tanks keep appearing at autojumbles and baffle restorers.

C20. Final versions of the M21 were supplied with an alternator mounted on the end of the crankshaft. But when the last batch left the Small Heath factory in 1963 the age of the hard slogging single cylinder side valve BSA was at an end.